FEARLESS FAITH

Life After Cancer:
HOW TO SURVIVE A LIFE TSUNAMI AND WIN

DR. MISSY JOHNSON
#1 BESTSELLING AUTHOR

FEARLESS FAITH

Life After Cancer
HOW TO SURVIVE A LIFE TSUNAMI AND WIN

by DR. MISSY JOHNSON

Copyright © 2018 Be Fearless Be Free LLC
P.O. Box 312 Interstate 94 Belleville, Michigan 48111
Website: www.askdrmissy.com

All rights reserved. This is a work of non-fiction. No part of this publication may be reproduced, stored in a retrieval system, or transmitted in any form or by any means—electronic, mechanical, photocopy, recording, or any other—except for brief quotations in printed reviews, without the prior permission of the author/publisher.

ISBN-13:   978-0-9899802-1-0
Photography: Bre'ann White
Cover Design: Melodye Hunter
Editing: Gloria Palmer Walker

Dr. Missy Johnson can be contacted at:
P.O. Box 312 Interstate 94 Belleville, Michigan 48111

Telephone: (313)279-8712
Email: askdrmissy@gmail.com
Website: www.askdrmissy.com
Facebook: AskDrMissy
Instagram: @AskDrMissy
Twitter: @AskDrMissy

Dedications

This book is dedicated to my husband, Lee Johnson, who stood by my side and never gave up on me or our marriage. He is the glue! I not only love him but I am in love with my husband after all these years.

To my son, Mychael, who loves his mom unconditionally. He is the apple of my eye.

To Snuggles and Dymond, who were my healing dogs through all my near-death experiences.

To my mother, who prayed for me.

To my sisters, nieces, and nephews, too many to name: I love them dearly.

A very special dedication to my Aunt Mattie Jackson, who is no longer with me, but without her, there wouldn't have been a Fearless Faith movement or a Fearless Women Rock. She passed her mantle of serving to me and I will keep her legacy alive.

Acknowledgements

I would like to thank some very special ladies who have worked by my side without pay and volunteered their time to help me fulfill the divine assignment. It would not have been possible without Simone, Michelle, Arnissa, and Brenda.

I am grateful for: The many doctors I encountered who worked diligently to keep me alive during my near-death experiences; my colleagues—Kristen, Ginger, Klo, and Terry (Snaky)—who loved me and checked on my continually; my friends who took me to chemo and drove a few miles to see if I needed anything—Andrea and Michelle; my spiritual mother, Donna S., who prayed for me endlessly, and my spiritual sister, Donna I; Apostle Larita, Dr. Yolanda, and Dominion International, who kept me on the prayer wall at all times; my pastor, Bishop Brooks, and the family (Faithe) who always checked on me.

I am also grateful for: Heidi, Stacey, Chuckie, Maryann, Brian, Kim, Gavin, Stacy, Rob, and Lisa, who never let us go without a meal; all the coaches, teachers, and trainers, especially Tressa, who loved me and believed in me beyond my wildest dreams; most importantly, every person who ever prayed for me during these challenging years; Dr. Stubbs and the Fearless Women Rock family, who believed in the assignment. They kept me going and they are the wind beneath my wings. This book would not be possible without them.

FEARLESS FAITH

Life After Cancer:
How to Survive a Tsunami and Win

BE FEARLESS BE FREE PUBLISHING - DETROIT

Table of Contents

Dedications	5
Acknowledgements	7
Chapter One: Faith is the Sixth Sense	14
Chapter Two: The Tsunami of Marriage	23
Chapter Three: The Tsunami of Facing Near-Death-Challenges	36
Chapter Four: The Tsunami Job (Career)	47
Chapter Five: The Tsunami of Family	58
Chapter Six: The Tsunami of Church Hurt	68
Chapter Seven: The Tsunami of Children	78
Chapter Eight: The Tsunami of Starting Over	88
Chapter Nine: The Tsunami of Being Accepted	100
Chapter Ten: The Tsunami of the NFL Club (No Friends or Family Left)	111
Chapter Eleven: The Tsunami of Identity	122
Chapter Twelve: The Tsunami of Being Single	132
Meet the Author	141

Chapter One:

FAITH IS THE SIXTH SENSE

Faith is taking the first step even when you don't see the whole staircase. **Martin Luther King Jr.**

Being a church girl from Detroit, it was expected that my sisters and I attend all church services and memorize Bible verses and Bible stories. We had to be the exception to the rule because our mom and aunt were Sunday School teachers. We also were taught the power of vision, faith, and the power to trust God in any situation.

During the middle of the week, we were tested on how many chapters we knew and the Bible verses of the week. We also had to learn one Bible story a month. That was a lot of pressure for us kids. The reason for the pressure was, if none of the other kids from Sunday School memorized the Bible verses of the week, we were asked to step in as a backup and repeat them so the Sunday School teacher wouldn't be embarrassed.

For me, it was a love-hate relationship to remember the Bible verses every week. However, I also kind of enjoyed it because I liked to compete; it was my strength. In addition, my aunt or mom would always add an extra dollar or two to my allowance for helping the kids out. Even more important, I liked to win. Plus, it made my mother and aunt proud of me, and no embarrassment was brought on the family. It was a joy to be the smartest kid in the Sunday School class and that was what I became known for. The irony was I started to love memorizing Bible verses and stories. It helped me to increase my faith, trust in God, and understand the power of vision.

One of my favorite Bible stories was the story about Moses parting the Red Sea. Even though I fully did not understand at the time, the story intrigued me. As a child, it baffled me for years how this man could take a stick, separate the Sea, and have the people walk on dry land. Then, once they got over to the other side, the Sea closed up. Think of my imagination as a child reading this.

Being a church girl raised by traditional parents from the old school, I just went along with the program because nobody questioned my mom, aunt, God, or Moses. However, I always wondered how that had happened. Also, I was taught not to question God, and if I had, I probably would have gotten my butt whipped, so I just kept quiet—competing, winning, and getting extra money in my allowances.

It wasn't until I became an adult that I began to

question Bible verses and Bible stories. I even questioned my faith in God. One thing that puzzled me was how does God have the whole world in His hands and care about me? How could I have faith in a situation I could not see? And how could I trust God when I had trust issues with people? This weighed heavily on my heart for years.

As a child, I couldn't really challenge my mom or ask a question because that was considered disrespectful. As I became an adult, I started to have my own experiences about Bible verses and Bible stories, and I needed answers. There is a Scripture in the Bible that reminds me of this experience:

When I was a child, I spake as a child, I understood as a child, I thought as a child: but when I became a man, I put away childish things. 1 Corinthians 13:11 KJV

Well, childish things were put away. As an adult, I view the Bible verses and Bible stories differently, and I ask myself daily how can I apply what I learned as a child to my daily life without questioning God. One thing I did learn as a child was to honor God in every situation and to reverence His name.

As I began seeking God for myself, I started wondering what does faith really do. Is faith real, and can you see, touch, feel, hear, or taste faith? Even though I grew up in church, my belief about Bible stories and verse needed to be factual. I needed proof that faith is real.

One thing about me is I am an advocate of education

and most things in education can be proven—i.e., one plus one equals two—so, my education and church teaching conflicted, and I needed answers. What I've learned is, each individual in the world learns differently. Each person interprets information differently. What can be proven is that most people have experienced life through their five senses—taste, smell, touch, sight, and sound—which is a principle taught in school.

Once I started looking deeper into myself and all the traumatic experiences I'd endured, I discovered my faith had kept me alive, and therefore, I called it my sixth sense. That sixth sense is called Fearless Faith: the evidence of things not seen, my personal experiences through a divine connection with God.

After three near-death experiences, the Bible verses and stories carried my faith, and I did not even know it. When my five natural senses failed in some form or fashion due to health challenges or unexpected situations, the one "sense" that never shut down was my faith. It was dormant in my spirit because I'd never had to utilize it or exercise the power of faith from my own experiences until I was faced with near-death. Faith is the sixth sense that never fails or shut down.

If I may, let me be very transparent. I know this may be hard for some people to understand and I respect that. Faith being the sixth sense is my perspective, my learning, and the way God delivered the information to me. It is not to question theologians, scientists, or medical doctors. Some of you only know about my three percent chance of living, the car accident, or being in a coma for forty-seven days, thirty-one days in ICU, and sixty days in the hospital. However, there is more to the story.

As a young lady in Detroit, I faced many tsunamis, but faith was my sixth sense, and it kept me alive. A tsunami is a battle where you must fight for your life. It will keep you alive only if you trust God, have fearless faith, and believe. This book is called Fearless Faith for a reason. It really could have been called Faith Is My Sixth Sense, but because of the mountains I've faced, I had to become fearless.

Faith is the ingredient that covers and carry you through a multitude of unexpected life challenges. This book is not to impress you, but to impress upon you that we all have a measure of faith inside us. When all hope was gone, nobody was around me, and I was faced with real-life situations, it was my trust in God, my sixth sense called faith, and my fearless mindset from those Bible verses and Bible stories as a kid that carried me when I could not carry myself. It was my faith that protected me from going to prison for a crime I almost committed. What you don't know is that my family thought I would be dead or in jail by twenty-five, but I am still here. Oh, no, you don't know everything.

Faith kept me from catching a case in my twenties. Let me share a brief story to tell you how faith kept me. Being the oldest of three girls, I was known as the boss and considered the protector. If anyone came on my watch, it was going to be a problem, and I do mean anyone, including adults. One day I discovered some information on someone very close to me and the information wasn't favorable, so I went to investigate my finding, and what I found sent me into a spiral.

As the saying goes, if you start looking for something, you will find it, and I did. After the discovery, I called my boyfriend at that time and told him what I had discovered. I was devastated and began to go crazy, crying and out of control. I said I was going to kill that person because it was going to hurt my family.

I felt that I couldn't be the protector any more. I felt like a failure, and I was only in high school. He begged me not to do anything. I immediately stopped what I was doing and sped drove home to see what could I do. My boyfriend called me repeatedly, but I kept hanging up the phone because I was hurt, devastated, and didn't want to talk.

I arrived back home and started looking for a knife, a gun—anything I could find. Not long after I arrived home, the doorbell rang and it was the police. The police said they had received a call (when I wouldn't answer the phone) and asked if I was okay. I told them I was, but they weren't convinced. It just so happened my boyfriend pulled up minutes later. The police left my home, and my boyfriend begged me to calm down and to not do anything. After the police left, I was crying so hard because it hurt so bad. The pain was so difficult to bear.

After hours of screaming and him talking and praying with me, I decided to not do anything. My boyfriend talked to me about faith and how much I loved God and that He would fix it. Because my belief in God was so strong, I started calming down. It was a pivotal moment because the wrong choice would have changed my life completely, and I wouldn't be here writing this book. I am thankful that God never left me alone. I am thankful my sixth sense of faith was working for me, even though I had my questions. God will place people in your life even when you feel misunderstood or broken.

When people are hurt, they will do anything to stop the pain. After all was said and done, I did not want to catch a case or go to prison. Sometimes when it seems hopeless, we will result to anything to gain instant results to bury the pain. What I am saying to you is faith is your sixth sense. Fearless Faith is the compass. Trust in God is your guide.

As we journey together, I want you to remove all distractions that will hinder your belief in God. Embrace Fearless Faith, Life after Cancer, whatever your cancer may be. Know that cancer is a form of something designed to kill you, but your Fearless Faith won't allow it to take root in your mind, body, or spirit. To survive a life tsunami and win is the goal. You win because faith is your sixth sense.

One of my favorite Bible stories as a young church girl was Moses crossing the Red Sea. All I can remember from the movie The Ten Commandments is Moses holding the stick up and the Red Sea parted. As a young church girl, I thought Moses was God, but learned he wasn't. I didn't fully understand the story until my later years. It is a story I never will forget because of the little to no chance that these people could walk across a sea and no one would perish.

Now that I am older and wiser, I have my own Red Sea to cross and getting to the other side is the great challenge. Just like many of you, we all have Red Seas we must cross to get to the other side. It can happen at any stage of life and at any age.

So, when I say the tsunami of life, it is a series of Red Seas that hit you all at once without warning. A tsunami is a series of waves in a water body caused by the displacement of a large volume of water, generally in an ocean. Usually, when a tsunami hits, the survival rate is little to none. The subtitle of this book is Life After Cancer: How to Survive a Life Tsunami and Win. That means, you get hit with a series of Red Sea life challenges, one after another, or all at the same time. Your chances of survival will be little to none unless you have a sixth sense called faith.

To survive the tsunami in life, you must have Fearless Faith. But know this one thing: You will win because you have a sixth sense called faith with a Red Sea anointing. God always has a ram in the bush, like he had my boyfriend when I was about to make a wrong decision, and you will get to the other side.

One of the Scriptures I leaned on was: Trust in the LORD with all your heart and lean not on your own understanding; in all your ways submit to him, and he will make your paths straight. Proverbs 3:5-6 NIV

Truth be told, I trusted in the Lord, but lean not

on your own understanding was a tsunami. He will direct my path, I understood. So, what I did was I removed myself from my own understanding because it was depressing me. Some things we are not meant to understand, so when I removed that from my thought process, it released me from being stuck in myself. Please know that no matter what you go through, you will cross your Red Sea because you have a Red Sea anointing on your life. You will get to the other side because God has you covered.

In the next chapters, I will outline the life tsunamis I faced, ones you also may encounter. It is authentic truth and my personal takeaways on how to win. I pray you will apply these strategies so you can prepare for your tsunami before it occurs. Now, let's take action by writing out what your Red Sea anointing looks like. Trust God in the process and embrace your Fearless Faith.

Dear God,

I ask you to bless whomever is reading this chapter on faith being their sixth sense. I ask You to cover them as they go to the other side. I pray that You give them direction for them to see what it looks like, even though they still may be in their Red Sea. Give them the peace that passes all understanding, and guard their minds and hearts. It is so, in Jesus' name. Amen.

Chapter Two:
THE TSUNAMI OF MARRIAGE

Love never gives up, never loses faith, is always hopeful, and endures through every circumstance. **I Corinthians 13:7**

It was a Labor Day weekend when I married my soulmate. The day was beautiful, and my bridesmaids looked like supermodels. People questioned, asking me if they were my friends. I thought that was pretty crazy.

Talk about crazy, my sister was so emotional—because she knew I was marrying the nicest guy in the world and everybody loved him—she could barely finish her song, You Are So Beautiful To Me by Stevie Wonder.

The next thing that happened changed the atmosphere of the wedding.

Our son was also in the wedding, and at the time, he was four years old. He and my nephew were walking down the aisle and started fighting over who was going to carry the ring. To top it off, my maid of honor passed out and hit the floor, and the groomsmen ran to the other side to pick her up.

Everyone thought she was drunk because she was my hanging buddy back in the day, but she was exhausted from all the pre-bridal activities. After we saw she was okay, I looked at my husband, and he was crying. I asked him what was wrong and he said, "You are so beautiful to me." OMG! I responded by saying, "Thank you." It was beautiful, but I had to keep myself together because I did not want my makeup to run and mess up my pictures.

With all the distractions going on at our wedding, we finally did tie the knot. I am talking about the tsunami of marriage, right? We are going to get there; just hang with me.

Before we got married, we requested marriage counseling from the church, and it was great. However, there was one thing I did not reveal during the counseling. I loved my husband to pieces, but I did not know if I was truly in love with him. Sounds like a Facebook post, or maybe not. I married my husband because he was the father of our son and a great guy, and I believed he loved me dearly.

He was easy to love, and he came from good stock. That means he was very respectful, loved his mom, and was a family man. He was one of the few guys in my life I had a relationship with who worked a nine-to-five, not the drug dealer lifestyle. When he asked me what I wanted for a wedding gift, I said a red BMW. I asked and I got it. Yes, he was the bomb. Not bad for a person who worked a nine-to-five job. He was such a beautiful person—but was it enough?

Since I used to talk to guys in the streets, our first years were difficult because I was used to a particular style of living that a job couldn't provide. Paycheck living wasn't cutting it, but I wanted to stay married and legal because we had a son together.

During that time, we experienced significant challenges in our marriage, to the point I wanted to leave. Don't get it twisted: He was crazy too when provoked. We had huge arguments about anything and everything. One argument was so heated that I almost left, but I ended up staying. The argument was because I liked hanging out like I was still a single woman, running the streets. He loved staying home, watching movies. He liked home-cooked meals. I did prepare great meals, but when I didn't feel like it, no pots were on the stove. Therefore, he would have to go to his mom's house, cook himself, or eat sandwiches. At the end of the day or week, we made it through by God's grace. I don't know how, but we did.

One thing about me is, if I set my mind to it, I am

focused, and subsequently, I would do anything to keep my marriage together. Meaning, I stayed in my marriage for a few reasons. One reason was I did love him, and it meant a great deal to keep my family together. If I left, everyone would have said it was my fault. Another reason was I didn't want to be a statistic of a single mom raising her child by herself when I had a great man in the home, but was that enough?

As time went on, I started asking myself, "Why did I get married? Was my husband, baby's daddy, my friend? What did I get myself into? If I divorce him, everyone is going to think I am crazy," because we were considered the perfect couple. People often compared us to the Huxtables from the hit television show The Cosbys. On the outside, we looked marvelous, but on the inside, I was falling apart. I didn't know what love looked like or even if he was happy in the marriage. I was just trying to figure out my next steps and if I wanted to become a statistic.

One day, after a heated argument, I packed up our son because I wanted a divorce, and I went to stay with my friend who had a five-bedroom house. She was shocked when I asked her if I could stay there for a while to sort things out in my head. I packed my things while he was at work, left a note, and said I was out of the marriage. I wanted a divorce for many reasons—main one was confusion about being a good wife.

After he discovered I was gone, he called my family looking for me for days until he found out where I was. My friend told him I was staying with her and asked him to give me some time. Then he started calling me. We were civil; I just needed a break to figure out my next steps.

It wasn't until our son got sick that we saw each other again. We both went to the emergency room to find out he had a severe ear infection. We talked and he begged me to come back. I listened, but my focus was making sure our son was okay. After I left the hospital and went back to my friend's house, she said, "Girl, he loves you. Go home and work things out." So, I did. She also said, "You are always welcome here."

After I got back to the house, it took a minute for me to talk about why I'd left. We still were on different pages and I wanted to leave again, but I stayed because I didn't want our son to be a statistic and I loved my husband. We were just two people living in the same house but apart. Does that sound familiar? Do you know someone like that?

Years went by and our son grew up. I was proud because I'd keep my word to myself about our son not being a statistic; however, I became a statistic. You may ask, "Dr. Missy, what do you mean?" A woman in a marriage who was not alone but lonely; loved by a handsome husband, but who did not feel loved. That is what I call the tsunami of marriage. I felt like I was single, but I was married.

I often asked myself what does that look like, being in a marriage where you outgrow one another? It seemed like being in a marriage where you are going in different directions. It seemed like one person was growing and the other person wasn't. It looked like you've lost the meaning of what marriage is supposed to be and the vows you took were words on a paper.

While I was working on keeping our family together, l was losing my marriage, and therefore, I became a statistic in every area of my life. I believe my husband did as well. Neither one of us spoke on it, but you could feel the tension in our home. We respected one another, but definitely were on different pages.

It took years to figure out what was missing. One thing I discovered was our upbringing was different. My family believes in hugging, kissing, and wrapping their arms around you all the time. My husband's family is the less-emotional type. Therefore, I never knew if he really loved me or he just stayed with me because he didn't want to go back home. My husband is a very proud man and a gentle giant, so it was hard to figure out his emotions.

One thing I realized was, if I decided to go back home, it would not be easy, but it wasn't a problem. Or, I had plenty of friends whom I could crash at their houses until I was stable.

One of the major problems I had in my marriage that I couldn't figure out was why my husband had a communication problem. What I mean is, we had a communication problem in our marriage when it came to discussing marriage issues. He rarely told me he loved me, and when you come from a family that tells you they love you ten times a day, it was a serious adjustment—and I did not adjust.

I've learned throughout the years that his family loves unconditionally through their actions, not through their words. So, I might hear, "I love you," only once a year, and that was hard to live with. Later in the marriage, I pushed the card to communicate more and it was tough, but it happened without arguments. Through that process, I have eventually learned that my husband loves me deeply. Our issues also made me realize it wasn't entirely his fault. The thing I discovered about myself in my marriage was I was on a path of destruction, and I did not know what love looked like or what being a wife required. I just knew to cook and go to church; that was my idea of being a good wife.

One day I asked him if he loved me and he said yes. I asked him why he didn't tell me he loved me all the time, because that was what I was used to. He asked, "Haven't I shown you that I love you?" I didn't know what to say because, finally, we were having a conversation about love and marriage, and it was a little scary. I did not feel that "I love you" was needed by my husband because I rarely heard it. The tsunami of marriage is real.

It reminded me of the movie Wizard of Oz, the character of Dorothy, because she was always looking for someone to love and appreciate her. Dorothy kept running into people who would help her get to where she needed to be and feel love, but she did not think she was by her family. My husband was the person in my life whom every time I hit a bump in the road was always there, but I did not realize it. He was always right in front of my face, but I never saw it because I always expected him to be someone he was not, and I did not appreciate him for who he was in my life.

You see, when I was growing up, I didn't have an example of what a husband looks like. That was because my father was an alcoholic; he ran the streets. Growing up, the majority of my time, we attended church on Sunday morning, Sunday night, Tuesday Bible study, and Wednesday service. The only thing I knew was the church, and when I was home, my father was working. When he wasn't, most of the weekends, he would be drinking with his buddies, so I never knew what a husband looked like. I knew what a dad looked like, but not a husband.

That is no shade. It's a real-life story about my father. He is no longer with us, but one thing I can't take away from him is he was a provider. The crazy part about this whole thing was so is my husband. He is an excellent provider, just like my father was. Sometimes, I wondered if I'd married a man with my father's attributes.

With that being said, let me tell you my personal thoughts as a young church girl from Detroit. I never felt I was loved coming up. My dad provided for us, but I didn't know what love looked like. Church taught me that Jesus loves me because the Bible tells me so, but no man had told me he loved me. So, when I became an adult, I didn't know what love looked like as a husband or as a father, so I had to figure it out on my own. As you can see, I brought that into my adult life and also into my marriage subconsciously.

Ask yourself, What does love look like in your life?

What pictures of marriage did you see coming up? What are you bringing to the table in your marriage? I never asked myself these questions, so I repeated the cycle I'd learned.

In retrospect, I married a man who is a provider, but I wasn't looking for a provider. I never heard my father never tell my mother he loved her, and my husband had never told me he loved me unless I asked him.

Now, I am twenty-five years in the marriage, but I didn't start falling in love with my husband until the seventeenth year. You may ask, "What-in-the-heck did you do all those years?" I was trying to find out who I was in my marriage. I was trying to find myself in all of this.

After a near-death experience of a head-on collision in a car, with a car hitting me at sixty miles per hour, losing my memory for three months, and almost dying was when I started having an awakening of who my husband was. He took care of me when the pain was so great. The doctors gave me all kinds of pain medicine because my nerves had been damaged and I lost my memory for three months. I ended up having a closed-head injury, and when you asked me questions, I couldn't answer quickly because I was trying to respond.

One day I was sitting on the couch and my husband was sitting on the steps. The pain was so great that I couldn't tolerate any movement around me; it would cause me to get lightheaded. When I looked over, I asked him if he loved me. Tears rolled down his face and he said yes. I said, "You must love me," and left it like that because I did not want to process anything else. It was too much for my body and mind to handle.

After months of me recuperating, I came downstairs as he was cooking in the kitchen. I asked him if I could start calling him husband and he said yes. That was my first time calling him husband throughout all the years we had been married and meaning it. From that moment, I stopped calling him by his first name, and I started calling him my husband. That was the start of me feeling like I was married.

Twenty-five years of marriage and I still have a lot of learning to do, which may sound pretty crazy but I don't call him by his first name any more. I am in love with my husband. He has helped me to understand and has shown how to be a better wife. Do we still have arguments? Yes, we do, and we don't always come to a resolution of the argument; however, I make it my business not to go to bed angry.

We think about ways we can make each other better. I am more affectionate now, but God, please help me. I am more emotional, holding hands, hugging, and practicing kissing him—that is big for him, and it is work in progress. A tsunami of marriage takes much work, but one thing I can say about my husband: I love him dearly. He is my rock, he is my everything, and there's nothing I wouldn't do for him.

So, what is a winning strategy you may ask me, and how do you get a win in your marriage? To survive the tsunami of marriage, you must have Fearless Faith. Love your spouse unconditionally. Support his/

her ideas, even if you don't understand them. Always communicate and tell the truth. The key is to release your expectations of who you want them to be and appreciate them for who they are. I had no idea of what a husband should be, but I had to release all the ideas and expectations of what I thought my husband could be or should be.

I want you to write down everything you want your spouse to be, whether you currently have it in your marriage or not. Write down three things you're looking for in your spouse or future spouse. Pick one of the three things that are very important. Pray over it daily. Stop expecting God to give you everything on your list, but appreciate your spouse or future spouse for who they are. One of my favorite Bible verses is about love. You will need this when faced with a tsunami in your marriage.

Your winning strategy to survive life after a tsunami of marriage is to release your expectations of who you want them to be and appreciate them for who they are.

And now these three remain: faith, hope, and love. But the greatest of these is love. 1 Corinthians 13:13 NIV

Write your winning release story here.

Chapter Three:

THE TSUNAMI OF FACING NEAR-DEATH HEALTH CHALLENGES

Every great dream begins with a dreamer. Always remember, you have within you the strength, the patience, and the passion to reach for the stars to change the world. **Harriet Tubman**

It was April 17, 2017. I remember it like it was yesterday. I received a phone call saying I was the recipient of the President Barack Lifetime Achievement Award. The honor was nothing I could have imagined as a church girl from Detroit working with others to improve their lives and inform citizens about issues that can better their community. The award was based on my many years of volunteer community service in the community, church, and on the state level in Michigan, working with high school students who were in need of mentorship and coaching as they prepared for college.

One of my greatest experiences in my church was working with the kids. The strangest thing was I did not like kids. Being approached to work with kids by a woman who knew I did not like kids made me feel some kind of way. This woman happened to be my Aunt Mattie, the Sunday School teacher. If you ask anybody about her, they'll tell you, you couldn't say no if she asked you for a donation for the kids. She was the most loving and compassionate woman I have ever known, and she was my best friend in the world. Mattie Jackson is no longer with us, but her legacy lives within me. Mattie loved children, especially the little ones. She just had a way of making everyone smile.

One church event that Mattie did with the kids every year was a bus trip. It created some fun and balance for the kids at church. The bus trip was to the Cedar Point amusement park located in Ohio. One day she asked me to help her because she needed someone to count the money. I would tell her I don't like kids, and she would say just get the money from the parents. I did it because when you collect someone's money, you'd better be with someone you trust, and Aunt Mattie knew I could get the money. It was a fun time for the kids, parents, and everyone involved. We looked forward to the trip every year.

One year, the Cedar Point trip almost did not happen, but no one knew what was going on. Aunt Mattie had cancer, but she was still serving the kids in the church and making sure they had a good time. After a long battle with breast cancer, Aunt Mattie died. She and her daughter died twenty hours apart from breast cancer. It was the saddest day of my life. The tsunami of cancer is horrific, especially if you lose people you love at the same time.

Just days before she died, my mom called and said Aunt Mattie had stopped talking and could I visit her at the hospital. I had to prepare myself mentally for this visit. When I walked into the room, she was staring at me. It was hard because she did not look like herself. She sat up in the bed and asked me, "Are you ready for Cedar Point?" I looked at her in shock because she was talking. She asked, "Did you buy the ham for the kids?" I said yes. Those were her last words. Forty-eight hours later, she died, still thinking about helping others, and she passed that mantle to me. The tsunami of cancer.

After we buried her and her daughter at a double funeral, I asked God, "What do You want me to do?" I could barely attend church because the looks on the kids' face were almost too much to bear. That was my start of working in the church in a community development project, helping the children in elementary, junior high school, and high school to stay focused, and developing a mentorship program to help them graduate and enter college.

From there, I went into politics, and no one paid me. I just loved politics because there was so much information of which our citizens were unaware and we always need a voice in the community. It was a great experience, and I had the opportunity to make a difference and meet people in high positions. I ran for office in my city and held a political seat in my town. That was the start of my season in politics.

After years of working with my aunt and the kids, I developed a mentorship program called the Mattie Jackson Scholarship Fund. It was a program to help students transition from high school to college. I was determined to keep her legacy alive. With the help of a few people, I was able to send over one hundred students to college with scholarship money and things they needed to start college, and raised over eighty thousand dollars in cash that I distributed to them. No one paid me to do it. I just saw the need to help others. At heart, I am a community-oriented person, and I love working with kids and working in the community.

Now let's go back to the day after I received the President Obama Lifetime Achievement Award—April 18, 2017. I was working and decided to go see the doctor on my lunch break. The doctor's office was across the street and what happened next changed my whole world.

It was a mammogram appointment that takes thirty minutes. When the nurse came back, she said, "We need to take more pictures of your breasts." They took more pictures and ended up doing an ultrasound. I asked if I could get dressed because I had to get back to work. Suddenly, the doctor walked into the room and told me there was a high suspicion of breast cancer.

I was devastated. I said, "You have to be kidding me."

The doctor said, "We need you to meet with the breast cancer team ASAP."

I said no and left. I called my job and said I'd suddenly gotten ill and couldn't return to work. I didn't want to tell my husband because he had been through so much with me and I couldn't bear to tell him any more bad news. In the previous seven years, I'd experience several near-death experiences, was in a coma for forty-seven days with a three percent chance of living, and stayed in ICU for thirty-one days, with ten surgeries while in a coma. I never knew what had happened until I opened my eyes and my husband was there sitting next to me. Later he explained what had happened.

Five years ago, I was involved in a head-on collision at sixty miles an hour. I lost my memory for three months and suffered nerve damage. I also fell twelve feet at my house after getting a Christmas tree from my attic, and the roof collapsed on me. I was in a wheelchair for nine months with a cast from my thigh to my ankle. So, I felt telling my husband I had breast cancer was too much. I couldn't process it myself.

Well, I ended up telling him about the results of the ultrasound, but I told him I wasn't telling my family. I had just received the President Barack Obama Lifetime

Achievement Award, and we were all going out of town to a huge gala. I didn't want to bring any bad news to that event. I wanted my family to experience the celebration, and I would tell them when we got back. It was an excellent event, and my family was proud of me.

Once we got back to Detroit, I delivered the news to my family, and it was not received well because I had to start chemo the following week. I had to start preparing myself to go to the breast cancer center to talk to these doctors. At this point, I became angry with God. I know I'm a church girl from Detroit and we aren't supposed to say that, but I was angry because I felt like I'd had my share. After I stopped being angry, I asked God to forgive me.

God, if you allow me to live after this, I will do three things: I will go where you have me to go. I will do what you have me to do. I will say what you have me to say.

You know what I learned during this process of life: God knows what He's doing. God is building you, building your faith. Even when you're in it and you don't even know what-the-heck He's doing, you have to trust the process, and the process isn't easy.

Let me explain what cancer looks like behind the scenes. I lost a friendship of twenty-five years living with cancer. I lost who I was becoming because I was used to having blonde hair and big breasts define me. I could no longer wear high heel shoes because my bones were deteriorating because of the chemo. I was use to going places, getting on planes, and speaking life, and I couldn't do that any more because of the cancer.

It was difficult to have relations with my husband because my body was going through so many changes. I was losing my body, my hair, and my mind because of chemo brain. My marriage and family were a challenge, and I even broke relationships with some people because I decided I cut my hair live on Facebook.

It wasn't my intention, but it happened. I wanted people to know that even if you face a tsunami of cancer, you can still be president. Some people ostracized me when I did the Facebook video, but I said, "God, if I'm going to go through this thing, I'm not going to go through it alone because I want to be an inspiration to other women who have a life with cancer."

I've always said, you may not have cancer, but I believe everyone has a form of cancer—meaning there is something out to kill, destroy, and break up your destiny, your purpose, and steal your dreams.

I am a church girl straight outta Detroit, and Bible verses and stories have always been where I've found the peace that passes all understanding. So, when I thought about the woman with the issue of blood for twelve years, it was my safety net. She was talked about and despised by the people she cared about. She was considered an unclean woman, but she just knew, if she could get to Jesus, she would be made whole. I knew that despite everything I'd lost, God would make me whole. I lost a twenty-five-year relationship, but God replaced that old relationship with new relationships.

How the woman with the issue of blood pressed through the crowd to get to Jesus! Can you imagine the mindset she had after carrying something for twelve years?

That is what a tsunami of life with health challenges looks like in real time. The car accident, coma, and breast cancer were a series of things designed to take me out, but if I pressed through like the woman with the issue of blood, my faith would make me whole. I had no choice but to press through and have Fearless Faith because it had been only a couple of years previous that Aunt Mattie and her daughter had died back-to-back of breast cancer. When I was diagnosed, I said, "This is not how my story is going to end!"

The winning strategy is you have to press into your win. I'm going to say it again: It's time for you to press into your winning strategy. You may not have experienced a car accident, cancer, a coma, or had a three percent chance of living, but I can guarantee that you will be faced with a health challenge or someone close to you will. So, I'm going to give you the strategy for when you are faced with life after a health challenge.

Things will change and so will people, but you must learn to reset your life. When I was a teenager, I had a perfect body, but after I had been married for a little while, that body changed. I don't look like a twenty-one year old any more, have long, blonde hair—Chinese, Malaysian, or Indian Remy, thirty inches long—and my skin has changed and discolored due to chemo. But after all, I have been through, I still have my joy and peace, and I still look good.

When you have cancer, it does something to you I

can't even explain. I could have chosen to wear a wig while going through the cancer, but I chose not to because it felt like I'd lost my crown. I would go into my bathroom and look at all the hair I'd purchased over the years, and I just didn't want to wear it. I would look at my stomach, and it wasn't flat any more because my stomach was swollen from all the surgeries on my belly. I've been cut on so many times that I don't even have a navel.

You have to reset your mindset because the person you use to be physically is no longer there. You have to accept who you are today. That was so difficult for me because I was trying so hard to go back and get her, but she wasn't there any more physically. To reset your mindset, you will have to love on the person you are today. Start to love yourself without the wigs and without the makeup—MAC, Revlon, L'Oréal, or whatever makeup you wear. Love yourself where you are. You might even put a pair of high-heel shoes in your bag just so you can wear them for fifteen minutes. I do that often now and carry both heels and flats in my bag.

So, the strategy is to reset your mindset to survive a tsunami of cancer and win. Now here is where you do the work to get your winning strategy, but you must have Fearless Faith and trust the process. Write down three areas you desire to reset in your life. Remember, you aren't twenty-one any more. Health challenges will bring things into perspective, and you'll want to reset your life for longevity.

DR. MISSY JOHNSON

It may not be cancer, a car accident, or a coma, but something is out to kill your dreams, goals, and vision. resetting your mindset is the key when a tsunami attacks you personally. Pray over it daily. Focus and master three areas of your life at a time where you desire a reset of your mindset. Your winning strategy to survive life after a tsunami of health challenges is to reset.

I am reminded of a Scripture I learned from a little girl, but only as an adult, have I had a true revelation:

And now these three remain: faith, hope, and love. But the greatest of these is love. 1 Corinthians 13:13 NIV

Write your winning reset story here.

DR. MISSY JOHNSON

Chapter Four:

THE TSUNAMI OF YOUR JOB (CAREER)

The first step towards getting somewhere is to decide you're not going to stay where you are. **John Pierpont Morgan**

I want to start this chapter by asking how many jobs have you had in your life or career?

I started working when I was fifteen years old. Wait, no, I was actually in elementary school when I started working for myself. I was a candy distributor to the school, not for the school. I would go to the store to buy the candy for a nickel and sell it for a dime. I was known as the candy girl and I had a little crew.

One day I went to the candy store and the man had raised the price of the candy a nickel. It was now a dime, so I wasn't making any profit. Since I lived across the street from the store, the owner knew me because I frequented the store at least twice a day. There was a candy ban on the store by the school, so they couldn't sell candy in the morning during the school year to the students, but he still tried. When I saw the kids with candy, I told him to stop or I was going to tell the school what he was doing. But I made a deal: He could sell to me and I wouldn't tell anyone at the school, and also drop the price back down to a nickel for me only. It worked. That was my first job.

The reason I was able to sell the candy was because I had a position called the service girl, like a safety patrol for girls, and I was the captain. I got to choose what door I wanted to patrol, and of course, I chose the door closest to the store. That was my first job. You might say I've always been like a little street hustler because I was going to make my profit. After that experience, I started working at fifteen years old and have been working ever since. Time brought about new experiences, so I decided to attend college and stop working for a while. I went to college because I wanted to get away from my home.

There were a lot of things happening in my home, and I needed to get away. I am going to talk about that in the next chapter called The Tsunami of Family. School was easy, and academics and finding a job were never a challenge. Starting a new career brought opportunities; getting promotions, accolades, and awards came naturally. After all that schooling, I finally got my dream job working at a Forbes 100 company in Michigan, and it was one of the best jobs I've ever had. I started this job by working as a contract employee. A contract employee is defined as a person who works for a temporary agency, but they are not a direct hire of the parent company.

I busted my butt and worked for that company as a contract employee for nine years. Because I worked hard, someone in management took notice. He told me that if I wanted to get a direct-hire position, I had to finish my education and get my degree. So, I went to back to college, completed my degree, and was hired into the company as a full-time direct-hire employee. When I became a direct-hire employee, I kept getting promotion after promotion. That was because I was a hard worker. I stayed late and I did jobs nobody else wanted to do.

Not bad for a girl from Detroit who wanted to be the best she could be. From a little girl, I've always wanted to be on top and I like competition. Sometimes people feel intimidated when you work hard, get the attention, and receive a promotion.

Have you ever faced a tsunami on your job because of intimidation? I have, but initially, I didn't know what it looked like or who I was intimidating. It wasn't until one of my white counterparts approached me and he asked, "How did you get this job? Who are you sleeping with, and what pay grade are you?"

He thought I was screwing my way to the top, but I wasn't. I was just working very hard to make sure my timelines were met by the suppliers. The other thing my white counterpart didn't like was that everybody wanted me. I was a team player and I loved to see employees win.

I became the talk among the male employees and other higher-ranking employees, and he decided to get together a lynch mob to make me look like an incompetent employee. He felt intimidated by my color, pay scale, and my likeability with the other employees and a few of the higher-ups.

What do you do when somebody is trying to set you up on your job to get you out of there? I prayed and prayed, and I asked God to show me the way because it was getting tense. I even went to Human

Resources to let them know what was going on. When they looked at my file, they said, "You make significant money. We have great reviews about you from your past bosses. I don't understand." Those were also my sentiments; I didn't understand.

What I discovered was the tables were turning on me in front of my face, and I didn't even know it. I was facing a tsunami on my job, a series of things that were designed to take me out. Now we're talking about my money and that was an issue; those people were looking to sabotage my career.

Some people were setting me up to look like I was incompetent. People were going into the system and changing numbers for the productivity of my team. It was all a setup. I eventually saw what was happening, but Human Resources stepped out the picture. They were trying to sabotage me.

Now this next part I'm about to tell you about is something I've never told anyone. When it happened and they gave me the severance package, it was a day I will never forget. It was approximately three-fifteen and the shift was ending. By that time, all the employees were getting ready to go home.

I got a call on my two-way radio from my boss to meet him up front. I was like, "Why is he wanting me to meet him up front when I have to close out the system before the shift changes over?" I told him that, and he said, "Someone is going to close out your turn." I said okay and went up to the office.

By this time, all of them were gathered at the door because when you work in the plant, when the clock hits three-thirty—or whatever time your shift ends—people are ready to go home. I went into the big boss' office, and that's when they said that my work was low performance. I asked him, "How can it be low performance when I had some of the highest numbers in this plant?"

We proceeded to have a conversation, going back and forth. Then I looked on the table and there was a manila envelope. It was passed to me, and when I opened the envelope, it contained a buyout package. The big boss almost didn't want to give it to me, and the boss whom I felt was intimidated by me was the one who kept talking. I read it and said I wasn't taking it. My big boss was looking at me, letting the other boss speak. We went back and forth, and the next thing I knew,

Security was at the door. I was like, "Oh, my God."

I was being walked out with a severance package. The irony to this was many of my friends had experienced what happened, but when it happens to you, it's surreal. I really didn't see it coming. It was devastating to have gone to school, then put all my time and energy into a company, just to get walked out. The most hurtful and embarrassing part was it happened right in front of my employees. I saw some of my employees crying and I saw some of them saying, "Hit the road, Jack," because they were some of the employees who'd set it up to make sure my job was sabotaged.

I cried all the way home because I was trying to figure out in my head what had just happened; more so, I had to go home and tell my husband. Even though my husband had a good job, I was the one who'd always made the majority of the money, and I just didn't know what I was going to do. I was the breadwinner, and a decent severance package is not a consistent income.

I didn't have any money saved, so I was forced to take the buyout package. I started thinking about how I'd sacrificed and gone back to school for years to get to this point. To have it slapped back in my face hurt. I thought about the struggle of being on academic probation and working myself up to graduate with a 3.5 GPA. Then I ended up going to graduate school and graduating summa cum laude.

When I added up the student loans, time away from my family, time away from my husband, time away from myself so I could get the education I needed to pursue the career I wanted, then to find out my services were no longer required was devastating.

After I got home and told my husband what had happened, my husband was in disbelief. I couldn't even tell my family. I was in complete shock. I cried and I cried, and I hope you hear my tears in these words. I shut down and became depressed. How long was the money going to last? I still had things going on in my life I needed to resolve.

You see one of the things I needed to resolve was that I was still suffering from health challenges. I still had bills. I hadn't been a good steward over my money. I was use to just getting up, flying on a plane, going someplace. I was use to going to the store and spending five hundred dollars on groceries every week. I was use to getting my weave and my makeup done every week. My life was changing right before my eyes, and I had no resolution.

I didn't even know what was going to happen to my marriage. I thought my husband would be pissed, but to my surprise (Can hear my voice quivering as I'm writing this?), my husband said to me, "We're going to be all right."

I didn't know I was going to be all right. I'm talking about a series of tsunamis designed to kill me, to take me out, to destroy my future in my job or my career.

When I started coming out of my depression—no one even knew I had been depressed—I was still sick in my body from all the health challenges from before. I asked God, "Why did this happen to me again?"

How I'd gotten this job was only by the grace of God, so when I was let go, I was broken and wondering if God was punishing me for something. My friends told me they would never hire me back as a contract employee because I was black, but they wanted me to stay in contact.

Right before I had become a direct-hire, my boss came to me and said, "Can you come to my office for a minute?" I said yeah. He said, "Today is your birthday and I need you to go to your desk because you're going to get a phone call."

The call was from Human Resources. They said, "Your boss must like you. We are calling from Human Resources, and we normally don't do this, but we want to hire you directly and give you a thirty percent pay increase." They also said, "It's your birthday, and because it's your birthday and your boss thinks a lot of you, we want to offer you a position as a direct-hire, hiring you today. Come sign your paperwork."

So, you see when God opened a door for me to be a direct-hire, then that same door was closed on me ten years later because people felt intimidated by me, that was painful. I worked well with my employees and colleagues. I was just devastated, but one thing I want you to know: Even though the tsunami of this job was devastating, one of the most devastating things in my life, I still walked by faith and not by sight. I had to pray to God and just believe in His Word.

I have been young, and now am old; yet have I not seen the righteous forsaken, nor His seed begging bread.

DR. MISSY JOHNSON

Psalms 37:25 KJV

This Scripture really helped me because I had to believe in the Word even when it looked like all-hell had won against me.

REFLECTION is the winning strategy in this Fearless Faith, life after the cancer of losing your career, your job—how to survive a life tsunami and win. You win through reflection, so what I want you to do here is don't look at what you're going through right now. Don't look at the devastation it has caused you and your family or in your marriage, because if you are reading this part of my book, know that you can survive a tsunami of life if you'll reflect on the wins in your life. If you weren't winning in some areas of your life, you wouldn't be reading this book. I'm here because I had to reflect on where God has brought me from, and I want you to reflect on what He has brought you from.

Stop, pause, and reflect here on what God has brought you out of when it seemed like there was no way out. Reflect on the things He has brought you through. It might not be a career, but it may be your job. I know that to be true, but remember that reflecting and being thankful for what He has been to you is more important than the price of gold.

What I want you to do daily is write down three things about your job or future job that you are reflecting on. Pray about that and have Fearless Faith that God will bring you through.

REFLECTION *is your winning strategy.*

Write your winning reflection story here.

FEARLESS FAITH

Chapter Five:

THE TSUNAMI OF FAMILY

It doesn't matter where you are coming from. All that matters are where you are going. **Brian Tracy**

This chapter is going to be very transparent. What do you do when a tsunami hits you on the homefront? I am not here to embarrass anyone or offend anyone, but I'm here to tell my true personal experience of how a tsunami almost destroyed our family.

I am the oldest, with two sisters whom I love dearly and we are close. Therefore, my role as a big sister is to provide and protect, and I have taken it seriously. Growing up was a challenge because I was the one who protected my family. You may say, "Dr. Missy, it's a mother's job to protect, so why are you saying protect? What do you mean, protect your sisters?" Like I said, I'm going to be transparent.

Back in the day when I was in elementary school, my father was abusive to my mother. My father had a drinking problem. He would fight my mother a lot on the weekends after he got his check. My father also liked hanging in the streets with his buddies. When he wasn't drinking, he was the kindest person in the world, but when the weekends came, he was hell-on-wheels. The things I experienced during that time were hush-hush; don't tell anyone. I could never talk about it and I had to act like it had never happened. The physical and mental memories of those years I will always remember.

One day after a huge scene, I tried to commit suicide—not because I wanted to die, but to take the focus off the things that were taking place in our home. My mom found me, and I was rushed to the Psych ward of the hospital. My family thought I was crazy, but I was tired of all the fighting and all I had to deal with in the home. After the evaluation, they released me from the hospital. When I got home, it was business as usual—like nothing had happened.

I started wondering if I really wanted to die or if I really wanted to live. Internally, I felt like I was losing control and not protecting my family any more. The irony of this mess was the whole neighborhood knew what was happening, but some people in my family wanted to keep it a secret. I was tired of defending, fighting, and protecting when nobody was doing that for me.

As time went on and I attended high school, the fighting had stopped, but I was still miserable. I was still carrying a lot of pain from when all the abuse had been going on in my house. One day I decided the way to escape how I was feeling was to attend college. I was never pressed about going to college, but it was a way of escape for me—at least that was what I thought.

I attended a university in Michigan, and what happened there was I became a party girl. My grades dropped and I was put on academic probation for partying so much. I ended up going back home. No one checked on me to see how I was doing. I was just living on my own at school. So, while I was on Christmas break, I told my mom I wasn't going back to school, and she said, "Yes, you are!" She didn't believe me.

When it came time for me to go back to school, I didn't go back, and I was threatened to leave the house or find a job. I eventually found a job, and I found a rental property, moved out, and a friend and I moved in the house. One day I came home, and everything in the house was outside on the ground because I'd trusted this person because she was an older woman with two children. I was giving her my rent, but she was keeping the money, and we were evicted. She wasn't at the house, so I went to talk to people to see if I could store my furniture at their houses, but by the time I got back home, everything had been picked up off the street by strangers. I called family members to see if I could stay with them during this situation. No one would take me in. At that point, I became homeless. My sisters never really knew what had happened, and I couldn't tell them because I did not want them to worry about me.

At that point in my life, something happened, and I ended up losing my mind and going into the mental hospital because I had a breakdown. I don't remember how I got there, but when I talked to the psych nurse and doctor, they said I had been picked up off the street and taken to the mental hospital. I called my family, but no one would take my call. I was in the psych hospital with all these crazy people. I didn't know how I'd gotten there or why I was there. After thirty days in the mental hospital, they decided to release me, but I had nowhere to go because they'd found me on the street.

I had no clothes because, remember, I'd been evicted. The nurse said, "Baby, let me find you something to wear so you can get out of here." I told her I had no place to go. God always has someone in your life, and what she did was quietly collect money for me to take a cab to Detroit, back to my mom's house, since I had no money. When I got back to my mom's house, she let me in, but it was very awkward. I didn't say anything other than I would be quiet and find a job. In the Psych ward, I'd met an old woman who was so pretty, and I'd wondered why she was there.

It's bringing tears to my eyes because I can remember it like it was yesterday. I finally met her and she told me it wasn't her first time. She'd cut her wrist, neck, and ankles. She said, "Baby, whatever you're in here for, it doesn't matter to me. I just want you to make a promise to yourself that you will never come back in here again." I promised her, but what you don't know is that was my third time having a mental breakdown as a result of everything I'd gone through in my life. It wasn't just abuse I went through. I went through some other things in my life that destroyed me mentally and physically, so when I talk about protecting, that's a big word for me because no one protected me.

What I'd always wanted was to be loved, for someone to say I was worth it and to say I was enough. I went through so many things in elementary, junior high, and high school, and I still managed to be an all-A's and B's student. The only thing I had to hold on to was my academics; that was my strength. I never stopped loving anyone in my family, even though they never visited me when I was committed to any of the Psych wards. When I got back to my mom's house, my family never said anything to me, and I never held a grudge for what happened.

One thing my dad would always say after his binge drinking was: "I'm sorry. You're all I got and I love you. Y'all are all I got." I will never forget those words. My dad left an impression on me that no matter what you go through—whether you're an alcoholic, you've attempted suicide, or whatever you have done in your life—family is all you've got.

Now that I'm older, I look at my life and still carry that sentiment. I love my family, and hey, they're all I've got. I am a mother, married with a family, and the thing I take with me is, family is all I've got. It hasn't been an easy road for me to embrace my husband because I didn't know what a husband was supposed to do. It wasn't easy for me to be a mother or a wife because whatever I hadn't gotten, I wanted to make sure my child had and that my husband would provide it for our family.

I do not fault my mom for my upbringing, and I've just gotten to the place in my life that I understand that she couldn't give me what she was missing in her life. I believe because she was missing something in her life, she poured all of herself into the church.

God is good, so when I think about my family, I have to think about what my father poured into me and what my mother poured into me. My father poured into me how to always love your family, no matter what. My mother poured into me to love God because God loves me. We had so many tsunamis of the family in my upbringing that I brought the same tsunami into my marriage and family. I love my sisters dearly and they are my closest friends. I still protect them to this day.

Whomever is reading this book: I don't know what you've been through and I don't know what you've experienced in your life, but one thing I do know is, whatever you've experienced in your life as a young person, I promise you, if you don't seek God for guidance, you are going to bring those same issues to your family as an adult.

When you think of Fearless Faith, Life After Cancer, I want you to know how to survive life after the tsunami with your family.

Sometimes in life, the biggest pain you're going to have is with the people closest to you, the ones you love the most—family. What I'm asking you to do from my heart is not to blame them because they can only teach you what they have experienced. If they have not experienced anything in their lives, you cannot learn from them. Don't hold any grudges, don't be mad, and don't take it out on someone else in your family because of the things you have been through.

Yes, I've been in a mental institution three times. I have done a lot of crazy things, and you are going to get to read about some of those things in this book, but I want you to understand, when I talk about Fearless Faith life and a tsunami of the family, sometimes your family can be your worst tsunami.

I'm often reminded as a church girl in Detroit of the saying: The family that prays together stays together. I'm going to say that again because it needs to be said: *The family that prays together stays together.*

Were we always in the same room praying? No. Were we always in the same house praying? No. What I do know is my mother is a Christian woman, a prayer warrior, and non-controversial person. She taught us to pray when things were going on in the house.

God cares and prayers work are things to always remember when you are going through something in your family. Call on the name of Jesus and let Him restore the year of the cankerworm. Everything that was stolen from you or your childhood, let Him bring it back. Everything you brought into your adult family that's a tsunami, that thing that's trying to take you out—ask God to restore it.

Restore is your strategy to win in the tsunami of family. So, in talking about Fearless Faith, Life After Cancer, how to survive a life tsunami of the family, I want you to write down three things you want restored for your family, today, right now. I don't care if it's a little crazy. I don't care if you think it won't happen. It will happen if you'll have Fearless Faith and ask God to restore it. Ask God to give you the insight and the provision that the restoration is coming. Don't even think about it. God is a restorer.

My father is no longer with us, but God restored my relationship with my father. God restored the relationship with my mom. Before my father passed, he accepted Christ into his life. I have forgiven him for all the mental and physical abuse that was caused in our family. God restores relationships. He will restore your current family situation with your husband, restore your children, He will even restore you, and it doesn't matter where you in life because He cares about every situation. That is something I had to learn from my own personal life experience with trusting God.

Your winning strategy for a tsunami of family is restoration. Years pass, and we never get them back. God promises the impossible:

I will restore to you the years that the locust hath eaten.
Joel 2:25 KJV

Write your winning restoration story here.

67

FEARLESS FAITH

Chapter Six:

THE TSUNAMI OF CHURCH HURT

God can restore what is broken and change it into something amazing. All you need is faith. **Joel 2:25.**

Church hurt. This is a major tsunami. I know I'm about to step on some toes right now. I am a church girl from Detroit. I was raised in the church and I'm still at the same church. What I want you to take from this is that church hurt is real, and it happens on all levels. This is my personal story about church hurt.

It was the year of 2004, when my aunt was in charge of the Sunday School classes and a lot of other things in the church. She was the go-to person for the children's ministry and new member fellowship. I called her my Harriet Truman because she was so diligent, such a hard worker, and I miss her so much. Actually, she was my best friend. She had been through so much in her life, but you would never know it. She loved the church and she loved the children. She loved having fun. She knew church protocol, trained church leaders, and she knew how to testify. Talk about prayer warrior—she knew how to pray—and she was the coolest aunt I could ever want in this world. Her name is Mattie Jackson. I have to say her name because she was also the first healthcare nurse at the hospital.

Aunt Mattie is no longer with us. She died from breast cancer, and twenty-four hours later, her daughter also died from breast cancer. We ended up having a double funeral. I was in a state of shock because I just couldn't believe it was happening.

Sometimes, there's a shifting that occurs when someone dies. People change, and I started seeing how it affected the children in the church. I needed to do something. I believe I was being prepared for this moment the whole while long. Aunt Mattie is the very reason Fearless Women Rock exists. When she died, I felt like quitting. I would think about her every moment, but now that I have Fearless Faith, I help others who have felt like quitting. You can win if you'll apply my winning strategies.

Why would a good person who'd always helped everyone die? It wasn't until I looked around the church and saw all the sad faces on the children that

I knew I had to do something. I asked God after my aunt passed what was it He wanted me to do because I wanted to create a legacy honoring her so she would never be forgotten. That's when I started working with students, and I decided to start participating in all the youth groups. That was my way of leaving a legacy for Mattie Jackson.

I ended up joining two different youth groups. The kids loved me, but the leaders didn't. Talk about church hurt—here we go again. Remember, I'd been at this church all my life. We were pillars in this church. The kids loved me but the leaders didn't, and it was a form of intimidation. I didn't want to step on anyone's toes, so I stepped back with the hurt. I had asked God what I could do to leave a legacy for Mattie Jackson, and He'd told me to work with the kids again. I said to God, "The leadership has rejected me, so what are You talking about?" God never makes a mistake. Have you ever thought that God made a mistake? Tell the truth. Well, He didn't make a mistake.

So, I tried again to work with the youths. Sometimes, you have to create your own yellow brick road, and that's exactly what I did. My auntie had been in charge of the primaries. Then they had a youth leader in charge who also had the middle school students, but they didn't have anyone in charge of the high school students. That's when I stepped in to leave a legacy for Mattie Jackson, to create a program for high school students.

I created a legacy for Mattie Jackson, coaching and mentoring high school students to be the best students they could be as they moved into college, and it was a very successful program. I worked with the kids from September to June, and it was so successful that when they graduated, they were prepared to enter college and be successful students. The kids were expected to write an essay to get the scholarship money at the end of the program. We did a fundraising project, met weekly, and I did a lot of mentoring. It was so well-received that the following high school class couldn't wait until the old class left so they could come into the program.

This was about leaving a legacy for Mattie Jackson. At the end of the program, I ended up having a five-star dinner for them because all of them didn't have money and I didn't know if they would ever have a first-class experience like that again. I wish my aunt could have seen it; it would have made her very happy.

Not everyone received the program well. Some people would come to me and say, "Good job, Dr. Missy," but there were some who thought I was just doing too much. It really hurt my feelings because it was my time and my money that paid for these programs. In the end, the program eventually faded for different reasons, but the legacy for Mattie Jackson will live on forever.

I can go on and on about church hurt, but this is what I want to say about it. It is real and it hurts.

There are a lot of secrets kept in the church that I've never discussed, so there was no time for healing. Sometimes the people who hurt you in the church don't even know they've hurt you. It isn't a God problem;

it's a people problem. People in the church carry their hurt from other relationships and bring it to church. I really believe in my heart the dynamics of church hurt involve things that haven't been communicated.

I really believe leaders need empathy training in church hurt. People talk about church hurt outside the church, but they don't talk about church hurt inside the church. The Bible speaks about casting the first stone. If you aren't guilty of that, then cast the first stone. There needs to be a group of people in charge of communicating what happens within the church, a business model that reflect roles and responsibilities. If this was in place, when matters occur, communication can be delegated to the right people. The system needs to be universal throughout all churches. When this structure occurs, it doesn't solve all the problems, but you will know who the problem solvers are in the church. Because church hurt is real and nobody knows how to address or who to talk with, often it is swept under the pews with no resolution. People are still hurt, and it has caused a lot of people to stop going to church.

I believe church hurt needs to be addressed. When I was hurting, I had no one to confide in; there was no one to answer my questions. I was lost in the pain. In the times we are living in now, there is so much separatism going on in the church and people feel the church isn't needed, but that isn't true. We need the church!

Coming up in the church, there was no one I could call on when I needed someone to pray with, but every time I would go to the altar, I would have to repent of my sins to God. I believe to deal with church hurt, we not only need to repent to God, but we need to repent to ourselves. Yes, a lot of people in the pulpit are doing things they shouldn't do, but that isn't my business; that's God's business.

There are a lot of people who wish they had someone to talk to about church hurt who won't tell their business and who hurt them. Hurt is personal. You must ask God to forgive the person who hurt you. Also, ask the person who hurt you to forgive you so you'll have a clear conscience; if they don't, that's God's business. Your accountability to yourself is your primary responsibility because you have to learn to live with forgiving yourself first.

I wondered if the church hurt was something out to kill me and keep me away from the church, but I decided God Himself is bigger than church hurt. I had to let go and let God heal my church hurt. I had to ask God to remove anything that would keep me from focusing on how big He is because I've learned whatever you focus on will consume you, and if I kept focusing on the church hurt while I was attending the church, it was going to consume me. I didn't want to be in the place of fellowship with people who constantly kept up confusion and church hurt, so I had to pray constantly and ask God to give me strength to survive church hurt.

I know Church hurt is real, but I know You look past my faults and You see my knee, so will You please remove this sting from me from church hurt so that I can focus on You, which is the bigger picture. Without any doubt, You will take away the pain of church hurt.

If you really want to live without church hurt, you have to let go and let God have His way. It doesn't mean it won't hurt you, it doesn't mean you aren't going to see that person, but what it does mean is, when you honestly and totally surrender to God the church hurt, that is when you start to win your tsunami. When you rewrite your story of church hurt, you will begin to see others in a different light because you are no longer focused on the hurt; you're now focused on the healing.

There's so much more I could say about church hurt because I have some stories to tell, but you only get some of those stories when you are with me on a personal level, but I did give you an example of church hurt.

This chapter is dedicated to Mattie Jackson, my aunt. I love her dearly. There wouldn't be a Fearless Women Rock without Mattie Jackson. There wouldn't be a mentoring program for high school students. Mattie Jackson is the Harriet Truman of my life, and her name will continue to live on in the church in the kids I work with. I have coached over seventy kids. Eighty percent of them have graduated from college, have high positions, and they have moved all over the country. That would make my aunt happy. The youth leaders working with them now don't understand my style. They are some of the same people who didn't accept me when I, therefore, had to create my own yellow brick road. Don't be discouraged when people don't understand your mission and the mantle placed on your life.

I'm reminded of a story in the Bible of a young man named David who tended his sheep, and as he was tending his sheep, he was the lesser of the brothers. But what God had in store for him was bigger than David could ever have imagined. And that's where I'm at in my life: Even though church hurt almost took me out of here, even though I was that little girl tending the sheep of the young people in high school in our church, He has something so much greater on my life than I have seen or have I heard.

Once you get on the other side of church hurt, your life will become less stressful because you are no longer focused on the thing that harmed you or kept you stuck. In actually, you will be able to help others who have or are currently experiencing church hurt. Because I am now on the other side, I can acknowledge church hurt is real, but you don't have to stay in your pain. More so, trust God to replace the old memories with new memories. Replace past hurts with new love, life, ideas, dreams, and goals.

Give me a clean heart that I may serve You, God.

I love God more than anything. God used the church hurt to further develop my faith, to trust Him even the more, so I could surrender totally. So, when you have a fear of Fearless Faith, Life After Cancer, something designed to take you out of here, your winning strategy is replace and restore. Ask God to restore you, to restore your mindset, to restore everything that looks like it was snatched from you. When I say restore, I mean regain everything that seems broken in your life.

Will you ask God for restoration in your life from church hurt? He will do it if you ask and surrender to His will.

Write your winning replace and restore story here.

77

Chapter Seven:

THE TSUNAMI OF CHILDREN

The greatest legacy one can pass on to one's children and grandchildren is a legacy of character and faith. We hope this plan will help you help you pass on the gift of faith to others in your life. **Billy Graham**

How many women have children or desire children? How many grandmothers have raised or assisted in raising other people's children for whatever reason? I believe many women will fall into one of these categories.

When I was growing up, I didn't want kids, quiet as it's kept. I didn't even like kids because they ask too many questions, especially the little ones. I like high school kids, ages thirteen and up. Because of my upbringing and everything I've gone through, I know how to give tough love. I believe kids in that age group go through so many changes that they need to be loved and for someone to give them tough love. Some of them have never felt they were loved. I am a doctor, a wife, and a mother to my handsome son Mychael.

You see my handsome son almost didn't make it. I was at the abortion clinic to abort another one, but this time, God spoke to me and said, "If you kill this one, I'm going to kill you." I looked around to see whose voice I'd heard. I didn't see anyone. I heard the voice again, a little bit louder and more convincing. "If you take this one, I'm going to take you!" After the second time, it scared me and I ran up out that clinic.

I told my friend what had happened and she said, "Girl, you're crazy. Go back and do what you need to do."

Well, the next day, just like clockwork, I got there at seven a.m. so I could be the first one in and the first one out. I knew the process like clockwork. This time I made it to the back, and they told me I was twenty-four weeks pregnant. I was so angry because I knew how this worked. 'How-in-the-heck am I twenty-four weeks pregnant?' Then I heard the voice again. "If you take this one, I'm going to take you."

Needless to say, today I have a handsome son who's smart, intelligent, and he's my everything. I named him Mychael because it means one who is like God and because I know God gave me my son. I know He kept my son for a reason.

You're probably wondering where the tsunami of children is going to take place in this story. Well, baby, I'm here to tell you, it took place for me when my son was in around the eighth grade. He started getting depressed because we were having back-to-back deaths in our family and because I was the rock of my family. I saw him going through things, but at the same time, I was trying to take care of everybody else. He began to withdraw into himself, and he wasn't that kind of young man.

When he went to college, he started experimenting with different kinds of drugs and different situations with people who were no good in his life who challenged him. Out of all the things a mother can experience with her children, suicide or attempted suicide is the worst. It's bringing me to tears to write about it. My son didn't feel like he was enough. He had his own demons he had to deal with. He's great today! He isn't on any drugs and he knows who he is.

The company he was keeping was unhealthy. They saw he was a good kid from the suburbs and he got abused by people who took his kindness for weakness. They used him up as much as they could, and as a praying mother, God was revealing to me what was going on. It was tearing me apart; it was tearing my marriage apart; it was tearing my son apart.

I remember it very clearly. It was the day my father died. My son and my father were very close, and our family almost couldn't handle the death of our father, especially my son. That was because a few years prior, my husband had lost his dad and it was devasting; it was like history was repeating itself. Mychael ran off to be with his friends to get high, but what happened the day after we buried my father was crazy.

    I got a call from someone who said, "You need to come to get your son or else we're going to kill somebody. Someone's going to die tonight." I couldn't tell my husband about the phone call I'd received, so I ended up saying I had to go someplace. We still had family in town for my father's funeral. I didn't tell him I was going to rescue our son.

    On my way to the location, I called my nephew and told him I was on my way. He said, "Auntie, that's not a place you need to be because somebody is going to get killed tonight." I told my nephew, "I'm going. If someone's going to die tonight, if it's going to be my son, I'm going to be there with him. They're going to have to take both of us out."

    Was it the ideal situation for me to be in? No. Should I have been there? No. Would my husband be mad? Yes. What people didn't understand was I have to live with myself, and if I had done nothing and something had happened, I would have to live with that regret for the rest of my life. I wasn't ready for that.

    When I got to the location, I entered a war zone. I told my son to get in the car now! My nephew was there, and I told him to get the keys to my son's car and take it someplace where he couldn't find it. His windows were busted out and everything, but I didn't care. I just wanted my son's car gone because when people are angry, they will do whatever. Before my son could get in my car, a big fight broke out with about twenty people, and my son was in the middle of that fight. What I did was I walked up in the crowd to get my son out of all those people.

A man I didn't know touched me on the shoulder and said, "You aren't supposed to be here and neither is your son. I've got this, and when I get done, I want you to go home and never come back."

He got my son and put him in the car, but before he could do that, my son took a whole bunch of pills. Less than twelve hours later, my son was rushed to the hospital for attempted suicide. He was in a coma for about three days, and when he came out of it, he didn't remember what had happened.

I told him, "I can't do this any more, so if you're going to go back to where I brought you out of, you're going to have to be there because I don't have the energy to get you out again, but if you aren't going back to that situation, I will bring you home."

He promised me he wasn't going back to that situation.

In order to help my son, I had to really be on my knees praying for strength and my family because my marriage was being affected, my life was being changed, and to look at my son and the things he was going through was killing me. But, I know a Man who can conquer anything, so even though I was very worried, I never doubted God. We sought counseling together and I never left him. We got help for him together. I got on the phone and called places and people who could help him, but the key with your children is they have to want to be helped. My son wanted to be helped.

I introduced him and reintroduced him to God. Even when he was in his situation with people and things, I always told him, "God's got you. You let go of God, but God never let go of you." When he was a little boy, I told him he was great, even when he wasn't in his right mind. Even when he was in a coma after attempting suicide, I spoke to his spirit man and told him he would survive. I told him, "You're great, and God has something in store for you."

I would rub the bottom of his feet and the doctor said, "How do you know to do that?"

I said, "To do what?"

"To rub the bottom of his feet."

"I'm just doing it."

"When you rub their feet, that's where the nerves are, and they can feel that motion all through their body."

All I could say was it was something God told me to do. One thing you have to remember when you're talking about a tsunami of your children: When a situation comes that's designed to take them out of here, to kill them, to destroy them, you have to keep God before them. You have to have the faith and the peace that passes all understanding, believing God will protect them.

God, I know he is Your child, but You gave him to me, so I'm asking You to bring peace to his heart and soul because You blessed me with him after several abortions.

Even though he was going through some crazy stuff with some crazy people, I never let go of God's unchanging hand. I kept asking God to intervene on behalf of his mind and his spirit because the mind is the playground for the devil. What I wanted to do was keep that fervent prayer going on for his mental stability. What I wanted to do was keep telling him that no matter what it looked like, God had his back. What I kept saying to him was, "I don't care how low you go, there's greatness inside you. You have a gift God has given you and it's time for you to exercise it, but you've got to go through some things and make up your mind it's God you're going to serve. God is great, and He's worthy to be praised, no matter what your situation looks like."

I'm just so thankful to have my son, who is in his right mind and who loves God more than anything. Sometimes, when he gets mad or disappointed, he gets mad with God. He says that God forgot about him.

I say, "Boy, God ain't forgot about; you forgot about Him. You can't negotiate with God; He isn't the negotiator. You have to do His will with everything you have. You can't play with God. He knows your heart before you even know what you want to do, so you have to figure out what side of the fence you're going to be on and stop trying to negotiate with God when things don't go right. Don't try to negotiate with God when it isn't going your way. Don't sit there and try to play God against your friends because you will fall short. That's just a part of life.

"Understand what the Bible says: But if God is with us, who can be against us? We are more than conquerors in Jesus Christ. You have to know that, greater is He that is in you than he that is in the world." These are the scriptures I was taught as a little girl, and I stand by them because the Word is true. The main thing I know is that God cannot lie. The Word says:

God is not a man, that He should lie, Nor a son of man, that He should repent. Has He said, and will He not do? Or has He spoken, and will He not make it good? Number 23:19 NKJV

That Scripture is a promise I stand on for my son. That's a promise I want you to stand on for your children or your grandchildren. That's a promise for mothers. Women who may not be able to bear children, you can help someone else's children. What I am talking about is a winning strategy for our children. We have to remember one thing: That strategy is our rescue plan for our children. Sometimes, we have to go back and rescue our children because of people they wrongly got connected with, or because of situations they got connected to. Nothing is wrong with rescuing our children because somebody had to rescue us. We all once were children ourselves.

Take a look back and think about the things you had to be rescued from. Did your parents ever have to rescue you from a life situation? Has a friend ever covered up something to protect you from something that wasn't in your favor? Once you start reminding yourself of situations you had to be rescued from or someone you know had to be rescued from, you will understand that Rescue is a winning strategy when you have children because of the love you have for them

Rescue is the winning strategy for Fearless Faith how to survive a life tsunami of children. Win, go back and get your children, and keep prayer over their lives. Have the Fearless Faith to believe they will be okay.

Train up a child in the way he should go, and when he is old he will not depart from it. Proverbs 22:6 NKJV

Write your winning rescue story here.

FEARLESS FAITH

Chapter Eight:
THE TSUNAMI OF STARTING OVER

I want every day to be a fresh start on expanding what is possible. **Oprah Winfrey**

Starting over is a scary thing to do, or at least it was scary for me. I've had to start over a lot of times in my life. Maybe you've had to start over before or know someone who has started over. Either way, a tsunami of starting over often will make or break you, but you must be vigilant and exercise Fearless Faith.

My life has faced many starting over points. I've started over in my career a few times. I've started over in my marriage a few times. I even started over after raising my son when he left home to go to college because

I was an empty nester. I even started over when my father died because I had to become the decision maker in the family and encountered greater responsibilities.

Sometimes people get stuck and they never start over because of the fear of failing, or they wonder if they can rebuild. Do you know anybody like that? Maybe it was you, maybe your mother, or maybe your sister. One thing I know for sure: Starting all over can feel like a cancer, something that's designed to take you out and leave you with no hope.

One of the many challenges I had in my life was starting over in my marriage. I have been married for twenty-five years, but I didn't fall in love with my husband until the seventeenth year. That was kind of crazy because I really didn't know what it looked like to be a wife with responsibilities or know how to take care of a man. Another time I started over was with my son when he left to attend school college and I became an empty nester. I really didn't know what to do with myself because my relationship with my son was to be a mother of taking care of him. It was my job to constantly make sure that whatever he needed to survive in his new world was available.

One of my biggest start overs was when I went back to school. I valued education very much; however, my reason for going to college was to escape life, not to get a degree. A degree was a bonus, and since I was smart, it wouldn't be challenging. I started college and met great friends. My homework in college was fairly easy, so I had to find something to occupy my time.

The school became my club. When I say I partied and partied, I partied like it was 1999.

I attended Eastern Michigan University, but most people thought I attended the University of Michigan because I was there all the time. My friends played sports at the University of Michigan, therefore, I hung out with the basketball players, and no, I did not sleep with them. I am not that kind of girl. After all that partying, my parents got a letter saying I was on academic probation. That was not good news.

After a few years of being out of school, I ended up going back to school; that meant starting over in my forties. It was difficult because I worked forty hours a week, was married and a mom with a four-year-old toddler son. The school was forty minutes away. The plan I created for myself was, after I got off work, I picked up my son from daycare. Then I wrapped him up in a blanket and took him to school with me every semester for two years. I was carrying fourteen-to-seventeen credits and working forty hours a week because I wanted to finish college.

Everyone thought I was crazy and wondered how I was doing it. I didn't have any help at any time because my husband, who has always been an excellent provider, had to keep the money flowing to take care of the household bills. Even he didn't understand. I told him to keep working, and I would figure it out.

One winter evening when I was coming home from school, my car hit a deer in the road, and before I knew anything, I had run on top of the deer at seventy-five miles an hour at eleven p.m. I just knew my car was all messed up on the bottom, but I was thankful my son and I were alive. I never told anyone but my husband. I thanked God we didn't die in the accident and my car was in excellent condition. That didn't stop me. I kept pushing because I'd started over, and when I start something, I finish it.

Yes, sometimes starting over is like a tsunami. It's a survival story, and who's going to win? The story of fear or the story of Fearless Faith? You have to remind yourself you are going to win.

I finally got that degree after two years of working forty hours a week and carrying seventeen credit hours for two years—winter, spring, summer, and fall. I got that degree. There was a reason behind me working so hard to get that degree. It was a promise I had made to myself.

It was important to me to complete my degree so I could finally apply for that job I'd always wanted. I applied for that job and got it. I traveled all over the country, met people, and built relationships everywhere. It was a great experience— until one day I had to start all over. That tsunami hit hard and almost took me out.

The job—my dream job—I'd worked so hard for offered me a buyout. I'd worked so hard and sacrificed so much—all that schooling and the student loans— and they offered me a buyout. I felt sold out. It was devastating; I didn't know what to do.

I had to start all over, and that was scary. My next frightening piece about starting over was I had to find a job. I had been making significant money and finding a job that paid the kind of money I'd been making was tough. 'Will I end up finding that job with the same money? Will people love me when I start working again? Or, will people start hating on me because I work at an automotive company that's one of the top-three companies in the world?'

Well, I found another job with a decent salary, but after I started working in my department, people there thought I had a country club mentality. Some of the employees weren't very accepting of me, and they started making up things on me, watching the time I came back from lunch. If I was one minute over my time, they reported me to the higher authorities. They watched the car I drove and how many spaces I parked away from the space the day before. They were trying to figure out why I'd left a top-three company to come there. What they didn't know was I'd been offered a buyout and I needed to get a check for my family to maintain our lifestyle. So, I had been offered a buyout from my previous company, and now it seemed like I was being sold out again by the people who worked around me. Needless to say, that company was going through financial challenges, and my services were no longer needed, with a severance. Here we go again.

Right before my position was eliminated, I didn't work most Fridays since my job had overseas assignments. Ironically, on that particular Friday, I received a phone call from my sister. She was in panic mode, saying, "Daddy fainted, and we need you to get to the house!"

I said, "I'm just getting off the plane. Can I meet you at the house?"

"No," she said. "Meet Mom at the hospital; she's taking Daddy there!"

When I arrived, I stated my name to the Emergency Room nurse, and she delivered the message to my mom. I was wondering why my mom was taking such a long time to come get me. She came through the Emergency Room door, looked at me, and said, "Your dad slipped away, but the doctors brought him back."

I looked at her like, 'Slipped away? What are you talking about?' "Take me to the back where he is." They took me to the back, and my dad was surrounded by all these doctors and nurses. I was looking at what-the-heck was going on, and my dad had a mask on his face. I remember it like it was yesterday. I asked my daddy, "What's wrong with you?" He shrugged his shoulders and said, "I don't know." That's something my daddy always said now that I'm thinking about it. I asked my dad, "Do you really know what's going on but you don't want to tell me because you don't want me to worry? Or don't you want me to know the truth?" In my mind, he didn't say anything because he was sleepy.

I hate the statement, "I don't know," because I think it's an out from a person who doesn't want to share the truth, or they're keeping something from you but don't want to hurt your feelings. Think about it: Is that the response you'll give yourself when you should be starting over? "I don't know what to do." "I don't know where to go." "I don't know what to say." "I just don't know! I don't know!"

Things started looking brighter for my dad. His vitals were coming back, and I was happy. Then, suddenly, the lights started flashing and a bell started ringing. They said they were going to have to shock him. I was looking to say, "What-in-the-heck is going on?" and they brought my father back again. This time the doctors said, "Call your family." I told my mom, "I'm not calling anyone. I don't know what's going on." Then the doctors pulled my mom and me to the side and told us my father was here now, but he could be gone any minute.

I was really over the top; it seemed like a bad dream. It was late evening when my sisters came to the hospital and Dad was resting. He'd started getting better, and because of that, they put him in a private room. We were happy. The next day, when we walked in his room, he was watching television. His favorite show of all time was Al Sharpton. I knew if my father was watching Al, he was going to get well. He was eating, talking, and a little weak, but himself.

The nurse came in the room and said, "Your dad is doing great. He is my best patient. Miraculously, he will be leaving me soon, but I enjoyed taking care of him. We are going to send him to the step-down unit, where patients prepare to go home."

I was like, "Awesome!" My daddy was smiling and everything; I was going to be okay. I told my daddy, "You scared us."

It was the next day. I was on my way to see my dad,

and I got a phone call saying my dad was in a coma. I couldn't believe what I was hearing. They had him on life support. It was a Sunday, and my mom and family were all at church. Twenty-four hours prior, my dad was going to a step-down unit and we were all excited, so to get the news that my dad was in a coma and on life support was really hard for me to believe.

I rushed up to the hospital to see for myself, and the picture I saw of my dad I will never forget it. I was the one who had to call my mom and tell her what was going on. After all the commotion, we had to make a decision about what we were going to do with my dad, but we were all in a state of shock because it was unbelievable.

The day came where we decided to take my dad off life support. My mom said she didn't want to be in the room when they took him off. I was in the room with the doctor and the clergy person, and I said, "I'm not leaving; I'm not going any place."

The doctor said, "Well, when he comes off the life support system, he won't be speaking."

I said okay, and they took him off the life support machine. My dad was looking at me when he said, "Missy, where is your mama?" I was like, "Oh my God!" My nephew was also in the room with me, and I told my nephew to get Mama.

My dad talked to me for thirty-five minutes, and all he said was, "I love you. I love you. I love you. I love you. I love you. I love you. I love you," until this last breath, with me holding his hand and looking into his green eyes. The doctor asked me to tell him to slow down because he needed to preserve his energy. I said, "Daddy, slow down; you're too excited." He slowed down but kept saying, "I love you. I love you. I love you."

I was holding his hand and looking in his eyes. The next thing I heard was the doctor said, "You did a great job, Missy."

I asked him, "What do you mean, I did a great job?"

The doctor said, "Your dad is gone."

I said, "How can he be gone? I'm looking directly into his eyes."

The doctor recorded the time of my dad's passing in that hospital room. I was puzzled, messed up, bewildered. What had happened right before my eyes? I didn't know my dad had gone while I was holding his hand.

There were many things I learned after my dad passed. I did not know at that time that my dad was the strong one in the family. Now, I had to step into his shoes and be the strength. I had to start over from where he'd left off with my family because now I am the rock in my family. I can tell you I can never fill his shoes, and starting over is challenging and tough. It isn't something you can prepare for, but you have to be willing to fill the shoes of the person who left a legacy. You must have Fearless Faith and know that God will bring you through.

So, you may ask, "Dr. Missy, what is the winning strategy to starting over?" What I can say is, I am thankful for every trial and every tribulation, even though I might not have liked it while I was going through it. Fearless Faith, life after starting over, how to survive starting over and winning is to restart your life.

The assignment on your life is never-ending. As long as you have breath in your body, you have another opportunity to restart your life. Right now, stop looking at what you've lost! Stop looking at other people's gains because you never know what they went through to get where they are.

If the truth be told, most of us aren't where we want to be in life, so stop beating yourself up. To win, you must get to a quiet place and write down three things you desire to restart in your life. Don't look at the "how" because the "how' isn't your business. Now that you have clearly defined your restart, start taking the steps you can to make it come true. Remember, you have to have Fearless Faith! How to win a tsunami of life after starting over is to restart, have Fearless Faith, and know God is doing a new thing in you, so restart.

Behold, I will do a new thing; now it shall spring forth; shall ye not know it? I will even make a way in the wilderness, and rivers in the desert. Isaiah 43:19 KJV

Write your winning restart story here.

FEARLESS FAITH

Chapter Nine:
THE TSUNAMI OF BEING ACCEPTED

Surround yourself with people who have dreams, desire and ambition; they will help you push for and realize your own. **Unknown**

In this chapter, I'm going to probably cry a lot because this baby right here of being accepted is HUGE! Right now, I am crying because this one nearly cost me everything.

You would never know Dr. Missy had been diagnosed with the Imposter's Syndrome. Let me explain what the Imposter Syndrome is. The Imposter Syndrome is when a person feels fraudulent, afraid, and does not feel like they are enough. It's when a person is constantly trying to fit into a tribe of people who really don't care about them. It's when a person is constantly chasing degrees, people, and things that would make them look better on the outside, but on the inside, they're a wreck—the Imposter Syndrome.

It may not be a clinically-specific definition, but you get the picture, or least I hope you do. Do you know anybody who suffered from or is suffering from the Imposter Syndrome, i.e., the fake person syndrome of not being accepted, not being enough? I do and her name is Dr. Missy Johnson. All my exterior workmanship, degrees, and accolades are authentic but, on the inside, I was suffocating who I really was. Let's use me as an example, in case you don't know anybody. Maybe the information I'm going to give you can help somebody.

Remember this is Fearless Faith, life after not being accepted, how to survive a tsunami of not being accepted and winning.

When I was a little girl, I loved going to school, but school was never really a challenge. My grades were straight A's and the teachers loved me. Basically, I could do my assignments very quickly and go do something else because I got bored really easy. It got to the point I started getting into mischievous things. It also got to the point I was expected to have straight-A's. So, all my life, I was the student who was the smart girl.

It got to the point that if I didn't get straight-A's, I wasn't accepted by others. Or people thought something was wrong with me or that I was rebelling to get attention. This was the girl who'd always gotten straight-A's, so if I got anything less than that, I also felt like I wasn't good enough or I wasn't being accepted. Needless to say, unaware, I brought that same concept into my adult life.

When I became an adult, I really started questioning myself. 'Am I good enough? Do people accept me?' Those were my thoughts, and I read books and attended personal development programs, going deep to find answers to my questions. I knew something was going on with me, but I didn't know what. I felt like I was having an identity crisis about who I wanted to become in life for myself, not what others wanted me to be.

Have you ever felt something was going on in your heart or your mind, but you really couldn't identify it because you didn't know what it was? Other people may feel the same way but not talk about it because they're ashamed, afraid they may be judged. That's why I have so many academic degrees—because I wanted to be accepted by others without judgment. I wanted to fit into their circle of friends.

Again, this is my story. Hopefully, someone will be blessed and it will help them to be courageous to step out from fear into Fearless Faith, so they will know they are good enough.

It was the year President Obama became president of the United States. I was at work when someone called me from his administration and asked me to talk about why I thought he should be president. This isn't a political topic; this is my personal experience. I said I believed he should be president because he cares about the automotive industry and because I'm a girl from Detroit whose family has worked in the automotive industry. When the automotive industry was collapsing, he supported Michigan and the automotive families and automotive companies in Michigan; that was very important to me.

The person who interviewed me was so inspired by what I said that he invited me and a guest to the inauguration of President Obama in Chicago because that was where the celebration would happen if he won. I thought it was a joke and I told him, "I have to work; I'm not coming there."

He said, "You would pass up this opportunity? Really?"

I still thought it was a joke, but to my surprise, it wasn't a joke. My husband and I were the guests of President Barack Obama as the forty-fourth president of the United States. It was an awesome experience, a memory I will forever cherish, but most of all, it was a something I never thought I'd see in my lifetime—a black man as president of the United States.

I'm getting to the point of not being accepted and not feeling like I'm good enough.

We enjoyed the occasion—all the radio and television networks, meeting Spike Lee, meeting Robin Roberts, having first class seats, being six feet from the forty-fourth president, and touching Oprah's hand (I will never forget her in her green dress). It was a day I will cherish for the rest of my life.

When we came back to Detroit, there was something

on my heart I just couldn't shake. It was all those young people of different races having the opportunity to work in jobs in the political arena. I didn't see a lot of persons of color, so I made it a life-long commitment to get involved in politics—not to get involved to impress people that I have another title, but to impress upon people that their voices matter.

The thing I get so passionate about is changing mindsets and contributing to the community to help other people live a better version of themselves, so what I did was call a few friends and asked them how could I get involved in politics. They told me and I ran for a trustee position and precinct delegate in the city where I lived.

There weren't a lot of people of color running for positions, so when I showed up at the meeting, it was like, "Who is that young black girl, and where did she come from?" I made a name for myself in that community. I hired a staff, and we went door-to-door, knocking and saying, "Vote for me."

I did it, but I was terrified the whole time—the Imposter Syndrome. Doors were closed in my face. There were doors that were never opened. There were some people who said, "Get off my porch." Nonetheless, I was persistent—yet, in the back of my mind, carrying the Imposter Syndrome that I was a fraud.

That's deep, ain't it? However, my passion was to change the environment of a culture, and I was feeling in my heart that someone had to do it. It was my Rosa

Parks moment. I went to bed with her and woke up with the Rosa Park movement and the Imposter Syndrome movement, but never told a soul.

It was November 4 , the day when people all over the country went to the poles to cast their ballot. President Barack Obama became the forty-fourth president of the United States. It was an exciting time for people of color. However, my story of not being accepted became real. I'm about to cry. I almost didn't go and vote because I just knew I was about to win.

I was the talk of the city. There was a little black girl who came out of nowhere and people were talking about her. She was about to be on the City Board. But, I got so afraid, I almost didn't vote. I didn't even go to the polls until six that evening. I stopped answering phone calls from my team because I was afraid of success and afraid I wouldn't be able to serve the people; they never knew.

When I saw the lines wrapped around the building because President Barack Obama had an opportunity to be the first black president and my name was on the same ballot, I was just too emotional. I didn't want to have a black president on the ballot, and I couldn't serve my people. What I discovered was I had a fear of success, so I deliberately sabotaged my own success

Well, I didn't win the trustee position and it was in the paper the next morning, but I did become a precinct delegate. I lost by two hundred fifty votes from being on the Trustee Board for the city. I felt like I wasn't good enough. I felt like the people wouldn't accept me because I was a little black girl in a white community.

One more story about not being accepted. I'm writing this book, and I have an anthology book coming out as well. I started a coaching business about eight years ago. I spent thousands and thousands and thousands of dollars, bankrupting my bank account. I bankrupted my 401k. I even bankrupted my mindset. I went from broke to bankrupt to broken.

Repeat, I went from broke to bankrupt to broken because I didn't feel like I was good enough to coach women. I didn't feel like I would make an impact. I didn't feel like my voice would be heard. I felt like I couldn't change the zip code. I didn't feel like I could change an area code. I didn't feel like I could change a city or country or continent. Hear me when I say this: I did not feel accepted; I did not feel like I was enough. I had to keep validating myself from a bachelor's degree to a master's degree to a doctoral degree. I was looking for validation.

Another thing that woke me up was it just wasn't enough. I went to go study the LSAT so I could become a lawyer. I said, "Maybe I can set some people free if I become a lawyer." But, when I started studying the LSAT, I said, "Wait a minute. What are you doing? I'm trying to be accepted. I'm trying to make myself feel like I'm good enough."

What do you do when you go from broke to bankrupt to broken? Everyone on the outside was looking at me, thinking I was so confident. On Facebook, people said I inspired them, but I needed inspiration. Sometimes, you need to hear you are good enough from other people. Sometimes you need to hear you're worth it. Can you tell me I mean something to you? Can you tell me you love me? Even on our jobs, our bosses are afraid to say you're doing a good job. I don't understand why we are tolerated but we aren't celebrated.

So, when I say it almost took me out of here, it did. When I say I was broke, I was! I emptied out my bank account—this is no lie—seeking validation and acceptance from those who needed it themselves. The coaching industry is beautiful, but it can be brutal. I was trying to validate myself by hanging out with the top industry leaders, buying every program, and going to every coach, and I figured if I got the programs, they would give me an opportunity to share the platforms with them. When I paid my money, they loved me, but when my money was no longer supporting their program, they dropped me. Yes, they knew my name, but that was about it.

When I say bankrupt, I bankrupted my 401k and my life savings. It might not make any sense to you, but I was so hungry to be accepted and so thirsty. I wanted to be a speaker and I wanted to be heard. I wanted to feel like I was enough and I would have paid any price for somebody to tell me I was. When it didn't happen, I was broke, bankrupt, disgusted, and broken. Can you hear my tears? Can you feel my pain? Do you know anybody like that? Or, is it you? It has taken me twenty years—twenty long years—and it has cost me a lot of money to find out I don't need your permission to be me.

    I could have lost my marriage. I'm shaking my head as I'm writing this because my husband loved me with my faults. He didn't leave me even when I messed up on the money. I think I might have left him—I'm just playing—but he didn't leave me even when I messed up everything. He didn't leave me when I started telling him I didn't feel like I was good enough for him. I didn't feel like I was a good enough wife. When nobody heard my voice or nobody heard my story, I felt like a fraud. I have all these degrees and no one's going to pay me. He heard my voice even though he didn't understand; he loved me anyway. I know he didn't understand the words, but he listened to my soul.

    That's why I listen to your soul to let you know you have Fearless Faith. When you feel like you aren't being accepted, it is a huge pill to swallow. It isn't a physical pill you take by mouth, but it is a pill you take by the heart. It's a mindset. Whatever you focus on will consume you. Not being accepted and keeping it on the inside of your heart, beats you up. Many people will never tell anyone about not feeling accepted.

    You must have Fearless Faith to survive a tsunami of not being not being accepted. I want to share with you today you have to have a winning strategy to win at the life of not being accepted. You must remove all mindsets. You must have "no-stinking thinking". You've carried this for so long about not being accepted. The devil will play on your thoughts to keep you stuck. He doesn't want you to see your future; he wants you to see your failures. Please know, to have a new mindset, you must think positive thoughts, you must get positive affirmations, and you must hang around positive people.

Write down three things you want to remove right now in your life that you can remove immediately. When I say remove, I mean three things that do not lift you higher, things that keep you sad. Whatever negative thoughts you dwell on control your mind. Today is trash day, so make sure you throw it out. "I'm not accepted" no longer serves you.

The winning strategy for not being accepted is to remove all distractions that no longer serve you and that means people and things.

For we do not wrestle against flesh and blood, but against principalities, against powers, against the rulers of the darkness of this age, against spiritual hosts of wickedness in the heavenly places. Ephesians 6:12 NKJV

Write your winning remove story here.

DR. MISSY JOHNSON

Chapter Ten:

THE TSUNAMI OF THE NFL CLUB (NO FRIENDS LEFT)

I can control my destiny, but not my fate. Destiny means there are opportunities to turn right or left, but fate is a one-way street. I believe we all have the choice as to whether we fulfil our destiny, but our fate is sealed. **Paulo Coelho**

People might be asking what the NFL Club is. Let me ask a question first: Do you have dreams, goals, vision, purpose, or a destiny? Who supports them? My answer would be my family and friends were the ones who supported my dreams, goals, vision, purpose, or destiny—until I ask them to invest. Let the church say Amen!

The NFL Club is no friends or family left to support your dreams, goals, vision, purpose, or destiny. What I found out was, if I sold a cake for four dollars or chicken dinners for ten dollars, my friends and family were a part of it, but when I started thinking bigger, when I started having massive dreams, when I started having a divine assignment, that's when my friends and family started looking at me saying, "What does she think she's doing?"

It's called getting uncomfortable. People will love on you so much when they can keep you within their circle, but when you start going into another circle, or another fish pond, they start feeling like you think you're better than they are, when that's really not the case. So, when you think of the NFL Club, it represents no friends or family left, and they no longer financially support you in your endeavors. If it's free, they're there, but if there's a fee, you don't see them. That's the NFL Club.

My story: I am a number-one bestselling author, Dr. Missy Johnson. I am the CEO of Fearless Faith. I have three books that I have published and a publishing company called Be Fearless Be Free. I travel all over the world to teach women how to become a speaker, coach, and author. Fearless Faith is composed of aspiring speakers and coaches and a book collaboration through the Fearless Women Rock Anthology project and the Fearless Leadership Academy. It is something God has placed on my heart, but most importantly, I show them how to step into their Fearless Faith so they can be the best version of themselves.

Everyone has a level of faith, but some don't know how to reach their Fearless Faith level. That is what I show and deliver to hundreds of thousands of people around the world, virtually or in person. I've been in a few life-and-death situations where I've had to fight for my life, but that breast cancer piece was one of the strongest things I've had to fight. When I was in a coma, forty-seven of my days were lost, but I wasn't aware of what was happening. However, with the cancer, I was fully aware, and it took almost everything from me because I was still healing from the previous near-death experience. Breast cancer is designed to kill you, but God . . .

I'm saying this to paint a picture for you. I was still healing from being in a coma for forty-seven days, having had ten surgeries, being in ICU for thirty-one days, having all kinds of tubes in my body, being cut open from my breastplate to my pelvis, then healing from the breast cancer. That NFL Club hit me like a ton of bricks, the no best friend left after twenty-five years. I wasn't in a position to fight for a best friend and my life at the same time. I was also facing other challenges behind the scenes, but this one I did not see coming and it almost killed me.

Fearless Faith had to operate at its highest level because this shocked everyone around me, especially my family.

You will discover that some people have motives when they become your friend and you are fully unaware because you are an authentic person. Sometimes, it isn't about you; it's about the emptiness they have in their lives. I prayed and I prayed and I prayed, and I asked God, "What happened? What did I do for this to happen to me?" Sometimes we look at it as if it's our fault. I started reevaluating my friendships and my relationships with people. I even questioned my current relationships. I questioned my marriage and my relationship with my family because that loss was devastating.

I'm not going to lie to you: To this day, it still leaves an empty space in my heart and it hurts. Some people say she really wasn't my friend anyway. Some people say people are here for a season or for a reason. Some of my ghetto friends—well, I'm not going to tell you what they said, but you can imagine. What I will say is that time heals all wounds. Surviving life in an NFL Club, no family or friends left, is a tough battle, but you must learn to forgive and keep moving.

After talking to God, I believe I'm still looking for answers, but I'm satisfied with where I am. What I also discovered is that in the church, they say new levels, new devils. I'm not even going to buy into that, even though I understand where they're coming from. It is true, like Sean Puffy Combs says, the more money you have, the more problems you have. I get it, but where I'm sitting in my life today, I learned I couldn't harbor bitterness-anger-hostility. I am not going to lie: I wanted to punch her in her face. You all might not think that would come from Dr. Missy, but I wasn't always saved and I will punch somebody in the face.

The thing that kept running through my mind was the movie The Color Purple and what Miss Sophia said to Miss Celie: "All my life I've had to fight." That was how I felt. All my life I've had to fight, and I wanted to confront her and make her feel the pain I felt. I wanted to punch her in the face. I was thinking that with my cancer, but I had no strength. When I became cancer-free, I still wanted to punch her in the face, but my Jesus wouldn't let me do it. But God!!!

It's a hard thing when you're trying to pursue your dreams, your goals, your vision, your purpose, and live your destiny when you are in a "no friends left in the community" situation. So, what do you do when you're in the no-friends-left zone and your finances are depleting? You have to start creating a plan to generate new income. You've got to go to a new community of people who are like-minded and start building your dreams, your goals, and your vision with them. There are great people out there who want the same things you desire and are willing to help you build your dreams. Do you give up? Do you throw in the towel? Do you stay stuck?

Let me tell you something. When your dreams, goals, and vision get so big that they scare you and you start talking about it, it will scare some people, and they will start leaving you by yourself. What you'd better do is pick your feet up and get on with your purpose; write your vision and make it plain.

It's lonely out there when you're building a dream, vision, goal, purpose, or a destiny. It's lonely out there and sometimes very long hours, and it's a scary thing, but you must have Fearless Faith, trust the process, and keep moving. Go find something that fills that space where you're lonely. I know for sure it's lonely when you are doing it all by yourself and trying to get what the next person has. Stop comparing yourself to others.

The NFL Club, no friends or family left, can be lonely, and you need to find something to fill that empty space in your life. That's what I discovered about my best friend. I don't know if I can still call her my best friend—really, I don't know what to call her—but what I can say is, she was there for me when I needed her.

Most of all, I no longer have anger or hostility. I don't want to punch her in the face any more. I might want to trip her—no, I'm just playing. I only wish the best for her. What I know for sure is you only live once. The suicide rate is at an all-time high, people! People are wearing smiles on their faces and killing themselves. People don't feel loved, or they feel lonely because they don't have any friends or family left.

I want to tell you is, you don't have to be in the NFL Club. Start doing things that fill the empty spaces in your life. Write down three areas where you feel like there's a void in your life and really ask God to help you to fill those voids. Start to love yourself unconditionally because God is love, and once you start seeking Him entirely and surrendering, the weight of loneliness will be lifted.

It's all a setup by the devil to keep you down and to keep you so scared, it will keep you stuck. God wants to see you rise. God wants to see you living your dreams, purpose, vision, and destiny. That's where He wants to see you today.

The winning strategy is to repair the old and replace people and things that no longer fit as you upgrade your life with new relationships. You may say, "I'm going to take my car to the car dealer; something was wrong." You leave your car to be repaired. When you pick it up, your vehicle should be properly repaired. What you don't know is, when you go to the car dealership, they check the inside, the motor, and they check the thing you said was wrong.

What I'm asking you to do is repair some things in your life that require your full attention. Leave loneliness where it belongs. Do not take it into your future. Write down three experiences where you feel the NFL Club has affected you. For example, it could be loneliness, leaving away from family and friends who no longer support you. It is your personal truth.

Now say, "I am leaving that mindset. I am not a loser; I am a winner." I want you to stay that to yourself every day until you believe it. "I am loved. I am lifted. I have dreams, goals, vision, values, and I have a destiny. Where I am going, whatever is missing in my life, God is going to fill that place. I might not understand how He's going to operate, but I trust and believe He's going to do what He said He's going to do because I serve a God who does not lie. He is not a man that He should lie, and because I trust Him with everything, He's going to repair the places where I've been hurt. He's going to make the crooked lane straight because I have Fearless Faith."

I learned how to survive a life tsunami of no friends left by knowing God is the Repairer of the breach and will never leave me alone. Repair and replace the old with new relationships; that is your winning strategy

And they that shall be of thee shall build the old waste places; thou shalt raise up the foundations of many generations, and thou shalt be called the repairer of the breach, the restorer of paths to dwell in. Isaiah 58:12 KJV

Cast all your anxiety on Him because He cares for you. 1 Peter 5:7 NIV

Write your winning repair story here.

FEARLESS FAITH

121

FEARLESS FAITH

Chapter Eleven:

THE TSUNAMI OF IDENTITY

A hero is someone who has given his or her life to something bigger than oneself. **Joseph Campbell**

Identity is a subject for the 21st century that I believe a lot of people have struggled with. I'm a church girl, and I was raised with a certain standard about the identity of a man and women. My belief is a woman and man should be together, but I do not crucify anyone who does not have the same belief as I do. I respect a person who does not believe how I believe, but do not crucify me because I don't believe as you do. Nevertheless, I love a person for who they are, not who they choose to be. However, I believe the tsunami of identity is more than just in physical relationships. The tsunami of identity lies within your heart.

In my life, I have faced many identity struggles about who I am, what I'm meant to do in life, how do I really see myself, and more importantly, how does God really see me.

How do you really see yourself? Have you ever ask yourself that question? In kindergarten, they ask what you want to be when you grow up. Teacher, fireman, and doctor are popular responses. It is instilled in us in kindergarten; people are pre-framing our identities. Then, when you get to middle school and high school, it's what are you going to college to be—still pre-framing us, giving us the identity of who we want to be, what we want to do, but not even touching the surface of you, what do you desire to be as adult now that you have achieved all these success in life.

Life has an external roadmap, or a picture of what we should look like in the future on the outside, but nobody has given us a roadmap from the inside out—from kindergarten to elementary to middle to high schools—of what we want to be on the inside. I call this the tsunami of an identity crisis. We focus so much on the identity of who we're sleeping with—female and male, male and male, female and female—and I'm not saying that isn't an issue, but what I am saying is that it is so much deeper than that. It is a soul journey.

For so long, my soul was screaming for help,

screaming to talk to somebody about how I felt in my heart. What I discovered was, with all the academic teaching and social ideas of who I am, they lacked the teaching of self and personal development. There are so many platforms of social influences within our society that sometimes people become less authentic about who they really are. Those platforms are great resources, but how you use them will determine how people perceive you in society. Sometimes, it is awesome, but sometimes it can be very negative. If you base how you feel about yourself based on people's opinions on these platforms, you could be dealing with a lack of personal identity.

That was me for a while. If people liked my pictures, people liked me, and if they didn't, something must be wrong. That was when I started working on building a stronger view of myself, and I discovered I didn't love me as much as I thought I did. It was based on the perception of what people thought about me, not what I thought about myself.

When you go to place a value or a price on a person's development, it doesn't really ring a bell for some people because there is none. Yes, I purchased personal development, self-love, get-rich-on-the-internet programs, etc., but I discovered it was really about life experiences and your values around those life experiences at the different stages in your life.

When you start observing you and the identity of what you want to do in life or who you want to become, it can be hard to focus on personal development or self-development because you have a family to feed, a home to maintain, bills to pay. Yet, on the inside, you're crying out for help, but you don't have the money to invest in your personal development because you're just trying to keep the family together. Am I talking to somebody, or do you know somebody who may be going through this?

Fearless Faith, life after cancer, how to survive a life tsunami of an identity crisis and win is achievable if you desire to commit yourself to change. What I'm telling you is it is possible, and there is a win for you.

One thing I've discovered coaching women and working with high school students is that everyone wears a mask. I remember coaching a group of high school students, and there was one beautiful young lady who was well-spoken and came from a great family. As their coach, it was my job to preparing them for the next level in their lives—college—as they transitioned out of high school. Every Sunday, we would have our coaching sessions, and in the sessions, we talked about personal and spiritual development.

One of the sessions focused on how you see yourself. I had a series of questions, then I asked them to repeat the questions and give me their responses. I went to the first young man and asked him how he saw himself, and he responded angrily. When he was responding, I could feel his anger, like he didn't want to be there. Sometimes when I saw him, I could tell he was angry, but I didn't want to label him.

As a side note, these sessions were strictly on a

volunteer basis for all students.

The big part about it was my students knew me, they loved me, and they trusted me. These were private sessions, and the parents weren't included. If I needed to go hard on them, they knew I would, and if I needed to love them, they knew I would. That was that Mattie Jackson spirit, the mantle that was passed to me.

Getting back to the young man, I asked him why he was so angry, and he said he was just angry. I asked again, "Boy, why are you so angry?" I told him, "No matter what it looks like, it's okay to be angry, but at this moment, you aren't going to be angry with Dr. Missy. We are going to love you." I proceeded to give him a hug, and at first, he resisted. Then he broke and I had the other students come over and hug on him.

As I'm writing this, I'm about to cry because something in him broke that released that anger. It was just a beautiful thing. You never know who needs love or who needs a hug. The tsunami of an identity crisis was he didn't believe someone could love him without any conditions, and that was why he tried to mask his anger.

Next, we had the beautiful young lady—smart, light-skinned, looked like a model. I asked her, "What are you holding back? Or, what do you need to release? How do you see yourself?" She responded with a couple of answers that were confident. Then I asked her, "Do you feel beautiful?" What happened next shocked me and the class. She burst out crying. I asked, "What's going on?"

What I found out was she felt like an ugly duckling. She felt ugly, not confident inside. Everyone always told her she was beautiful, but she didn't believe it. It was all a mask. The tsunami of identity. Everyone was always saying how beautiful and smart she was, but no one had a clue she felt like that, not even me. I approached that young lady, had her to look into my eyes, and repeat after me, "I am beautiful on the inside."

I asked her what was beautiful about her on the inside. I told her we weren't looking at who she was externally; we wanted to look at her heart. She couldn't answer the question, so I helped her, telling her what I saw was beautiful about her on the inside and had her to repeat after me.

Working with those two students on that day let me know many people have an identity crisis, and it isn't so much about the physical, but it's the internal and how they see themselves.

Many times, we compare ourselves to the situations we have experienced in life. We compare ourselves to people on television and in the videos. Nothing is wrong with either of them if they are sending a positive message. However, we have to be reminded that we matter! Being reminded sometimes hurts because we are looking to fill voids in our lives. What I've discovered is we are composed of mind, body, and spirit, and all three entities need to be aligned, functioning and moving together. In my personal experience, I discovered that, if any part of my mind-body-spirit wasn't congruent, there was something in my life that was off-balance.

I do not believe in perfect balance. However, I do believe the mind, body, and spirit can operate together to make sure we have peace about the situations in our lives. It doesn't mean I'll always agree with the situation, but I won't be so focused on one thing that it makes me incongruent in those areas. So, when you talk about a tsunami of an identity crisis, two things you must focus on: Love yourself first and seek God for guidance.

Like with the young man in my mentorship program, he had to be reminded he was loved. I don't know what his situation was, but I do know love casts away all fear and anger if you present it from an authentic place. The young lady in our group also had to be reminded that she was beautiful on the inside, not just the outside. Sometimes you have to remind people that their vision, goals, dreams, purpose, and destiny need to be realigned with who they desire to become in life.

As for me, my identity crisis was with math. I have received every degree at every level that is offered. I even ran for a political position. I've spent much money on my family and friends so they would hang out with me and say I was the bomb.com. I enjoyed it, until people started asking me for money out the blue. I had to tell people I wasn't the bank, but because I presented myself in a particular fashion, that was what they expected. It wasn't their fault. I had an identity crisis. So, when I said, "I'm not the bank," things changed.

When I started taking a deep dive into my spirit, my mind, and my body, and I started looking at my external identity and started searching for my internal identity,

I said, I think I need to stop being so financially free, giving them extra money, saying don't worry about, and buying all those coaching programs. When I did all that, baby, the game changed. People only wanted me because I could put their purchases on my charge, or I could give them loans they never paid back—the identity crisis.

Dr. Missy was in an identity crisis, but I had to remind myself to realize my goals, my dreams, my purpose, my destiny. I wanted to start looking at things that served my real purpose, dreams, vision, goals, destiny, and the divine assignment God has on my life. When I started doing those things, that's when I discovered that that was my winning strategy: reminding myself and relining the value that I matter.

Fearless Faith is how you survive an identity crisis. It's all about reminding yourself that you were created for a purpose. Align your values with what you want to become in life, taking the focus off your external situations and placing your focus on your internal situations, needs, and thoughts. That is your winning strategy. You must have Fearless Faith.

Remembrance is your winning strategy. Remind yourself of your values and that you were created for a purpose.

For You created my inmost being; You knit me together in my mother's womb. I praise You because I am fearfully and wonderfully made; Your works are wonderful, I know that full well. My frame was not hidden from You when I was made in the secret place, when I was woven together in the depths of the earth. Your eyes saw my unformed body; all the days ordained for me were written in Your book before one of them came to be. Psalm 139:13-16 NIV

Write your winning remembrance story here.

FEARLESS FAITH

Chapter Twelve:

THE TSUNAMI OF BEING SINGLE

You define your own life. Don't let other people write your script. **Oprah Winfrey**

Let me define being single in this chapter because it can have a variety of meanings, depending on how you apply the word. Webster's dictionary describes single as a person or thing being separate. In this chapter, it is necessary that I place specific criteria on being single because the term can be applied to many people and to many things. The most-common meaning of being single is a person who is not in a relationship with another human being. That characteristic is very true; however, the tsunami of being single is as Webster's dictionary defines it above. Many things in your life are separate due to a series of situations, a circumstance, or an individual. The question I have is: Have you ever looked at it that way?

    Even though I was married, I was a married single woman for a long time. Also, though I had a business, I was a single business owner for a long time. Even though I had lots of accolades and degrees behind my name, I still felt single within myself. I couldn't share that with anyone else because they wouldn't have understood. You may say. "Dr. Missy, that sounds crazy," but what I'm telling you is the truth, the truth that I lived in and hid in my heart. The tsunami of being single was a part of my life, in every area of my life.

    Take a look at me being married-but-single. Sometimes, we as wives live in the same house with our spouses, but we're going in different directions. Have you ever heard the term, one individual is growing faster than the other? Well, that was me. I was growing in leaps and bounds, personal and spiritual development, but my husband wasn't growing as fast as I was, and therefore, I felt single. I felt like I had left him behind where I was going. I couldn't explain it to him because I felt he wouldn't be able to process where I was going in my life, in my business, and in my spiritual development. There were many days that he kept it in, but I saw it on his face that he wasn't happy. There were many days I wanted to talk to him, but I knew it would start an argument that I just didn't have the time or the energy for.

I would always pray and say, "Lord, I want to bring my husband along in my development in different areas, but he isn't going to understand because things are changing and it looks like I'm leaving him out." I probably was, but not intentionally. It was an assignment on my life that I had to run the course with. I was married-but-single—living in the same city, same zip code, same area code, same household, and same bed.

It was in the middle of September when I married my husband. Believe it or not, I cooked for us. I didn't like to cook, but I cook because it pleased him. He loved to watch movies. I didn't, but I watched the movies because it pleased him. We loved to travel together and we had great times together on our vacations. That was something we had in common.

As time went on, I finished my undergraduate degree and decided to go back to obtain my master's and doctorate degrees. It was hard, but I did it, and my husband supported me. While in graduate school, I had a fall, but managed to earn a degree while I was in a wheelchair. I fell twelve feet in my house because the roof collapsed on me and I couldn't walk for nine months, but I was committed to getting that degree. I was committed that I was going to cross that stage even if I had to crawl.

One day, my husband and I had a conversation about education. He said to me, "You have all these degrees. What are you going to do with them? You can't even find a good job with those degrees."

I was totally shocked by that statement because I

thought he was supportive of me going to school. What I discovered was I was outgrowing him when it came to education. That was the first time I discovered he thought differently about me going to school. I thought he was happy, but I discovered I was outgrowing him academically, and he wanted to see the income match the education I had invested in.

To make it worse, I started working in my church with high school kids because my aunt had died and I saw the emptiness on their faces. I asked God to help me be a light in their life, so I mentored the high school students for six years. The irony of that was the parents started asking me to mentor and coach them also, to my surprise, and that was the start of coaching the women.

I'm still talking about being married-but-single. Now it was looking like I was really outgrowing him. I was coaching students and coaching women. Where did he fit in all of this? I guess you could say my husband felt like he was married-but-single also. At the time, I couldn't put my finger on it and I really did not want to. I had an attitude because he wasn't supporting me like I thought he had been in all of my education. I thought it would make him happy but, deep down inside, it didn't. The question I had was: Was I married-but-single, was he married-but-single, or were we both married-but-single?

I had to start facing the fact that I was married-but-single and I didn't want to be a part of it any longer. I wanted to get out of the marriage because I couldn't be with a man who wasn't supportive of me in everything

I did. In my business, I was mentoring women and traveling all over the country. My husband wasn't saying much about me doing this, but every time I came home, he had an attitude about me traveling. He wouldn't say anything to me, but it was definitely causing a break in our marriage.

Some women are single, they don't have a spouse, but something is still holding them back from living out their purpose. If you're married and have dreams of building a massive business like I did, being married-but-single isn't going to work. You're going to have to come up with some kind of plan with your spouse for you to stay together, then you have to work together to keep the marriage going. You cannot be married and single. The business is going to collapse and your marriage will fall through the cracks. From personal experience, you're either going to have to choose your marriage or choose to be by yourself.

As far as women who are single and who don't have a spouse, what I learned from my friends and family is loneliness can be the cause of suicide attempts. I know many women who cry at night because they want someone to lie in the bed with them. They want someone to talk to and they get tired of doing things by themselves. This applies to married-but-single women—nobody to turn to, to help you if something falls through the cracks.

If you are a single mother or a single parent, and your husband has died or the child's father isn't involved in the child's life, being single can be a tough thing to handle. The reason I know is I have friends who have been so lonely that they weep at night. I have friends who are single mothers, and they do it all by themselves. They call me on the phone and tell me they're lonely. I pray for women who can't have children, I pray for single parents who are raising their children by themselves, and I really pray for women and men who are experiencing singleness and loneliness.

I cannot say I have been alone—without a physical body next to me—but I have been single with a physical body next to me, and I really don't know which one is worse.

There is a winning strategy. The Bible says God will not leave you comfortless. That's what the Word says. I'm no longer married-but-single because I have chosen to not be single in my marriage. It is exciting and I thank God for working on us to keep our marriage together. One of the first things I did after I realized I was falling in love with my husband was I cried. I never thought, after being married for seventeen years, that I would say, "I am in love with my husband." It just happened and we are in love. It feels weird but great!

The first thing I had to do was go to God and ask Him to take away anything I had done in my life that had offended anyone and to remove anything in me I didn't understand so I could be a better wife.

The second thing I had to do was make myself get involved in my marriage. Just because I was married didn't mean I was always involved. There are a lot of people who live in the same house who don't communicate with one another. They share the same bed, but they don't even talk to one another. That thing is real; I'm just making it plain. You see, I've been mentoring and coaching women for a long time, but I hadn't been communicating with my husband how I felt. He was not open initially, but later, after several talks, he started listening. What I had to decide for myself was, if my husband left me, would I be okay with being single?

You have to get clarity on your position in the marriage. If you're looking for happiness in other people, baby, you won't find it. If you're looking for somebody to be your everything, they aren't out there. What you have to do is get to the point where you love yourself unconditionally and you don't need a man or a woman to validate you. Love yourself so much that when people come around you, they see the love in your heart. Stop being so thirsty for someone else to fill the dry places in your life. Ask God to bless you with a husband or to bless you with a wife. He will supply all your needs if you stay in the Word and stay on your knees.

The winning strategy to beating the tsunami of being single is Fearless Faith. Reflect on everything God has brought you through. Start reclaiming everything He's going to take you to in your personal life and trust the process. It won't be easy, I promise you that, but stay the course and keep your eyes on the prize even though you aren't there yet. As you reflect, remember, and reclaim your past, your present, and your future, and step into the blueprint of who God created you to be, know that He knows the plans He has for you. You may not understand or see it now, but believe, do the work, and stay positive and prayerful.

Rewrite your story about the tsunami of being single. Write your story about your future and how bright it appears. The how to survive being single tsunami's winning strategy is to rewrite your story of being single.

Write your winning rewrite story here.

DR. MISSY JOHNSON

Meet the Author

Dr. Missy Johnson is an award-winning, international, number-one bestselling author, speaker, and Break Free Coach with mastery in personal and leadership development. Dr. Missy has a remarkable story and is considered by her clients as a lightworker for the GEN-X women.

Dr. Missy is the founder of CTC Personal Development Institute, an organization that shows women in corporate America how to redevelop, rebrand, and reposition themselves so they can transition from corporate America into their entrepreneurship and live life on their own terms. The business model includes a blueprint that accelerates growth, mindset makeover, and entrepreneurship training as they enter into the new arena.

She is the CEO of Fearless Women Rock LLC, a platform created for women to share their courageous stories so they can leverage themselves to become speakers, coaches, and authors. Dr. Missy has been on the cover or featured in the Speaker's Magazine, Power Network Conference, NBC, ABC, Huffington Post, and Marie Claire, in addition to many other media, radio, and television outlets. She is a John Maxwell certified trainer and recipient of the President Barack Obama Lifetime Achievement Award and the Michigan Chronicle Women of Excellence 2018.

Dr. Missy is the survivor of a sixty-miles-per-hour head-on car collision, forty-seven days in a coma, and stage three breast cancer. Dr. Missy is releasing her new book Fearless Faith, Life After Cancer: How to Survive a Life Tsunami and Win. She is married to her devoted husband Lee. They share one son and reside outside Detroit, Michigan. Dr. Missy is available for speaking in the corporate arena and at church events.

www.ingramcontent.com/pod-product-compliance
Lightning Source LLC
Chambersburg PA
CBHW070430010526
44118CB00014B/1980